Vegetation Community Monitoring at Moores Creek National Battlefield, 2010

Natural Resource Data Series NPS/SECN/NRDS—2012/250

Michael W. Byrne and Sarah L. Corbett

USDI National Park Service
Southeast Coast Inventory and Monitoring Network
Cumberland Island National Seashore
101 Wheeler Street
Saint Marys, Georgia, 31558

and

Joseph C. DeVivo

USDI National Park Service
Southeast Coast Inventory and Monitoring Network
University of Georgia
160 Phoenix Road, Phillips Lab
Athens, Georgia, 30605

February 2012

U.S. Department of the Interior
National Park Service
Natural Resource Stewardship and Science
Fort Collins, Colorado

The National Park Service, Natural Resource Stewardship and Science office in Fort Collins, Colorado publishes a range of reports that address natural resource topics of interest and applicability to a broad audience in the National Park Service and others in natural resource management, including scientists, conservation and environmental constituencies, and the public.

The Natural Resource Data Series is intended for the timely release of basic data sets and data summaries. Care has been taken to assure accuracy of raw data values, but a thorough analysis and interpretation of the data has not been completed. Consequently, the initial analyses of data in this report are provisional and subject to change.

All manuscripts in the series receive the appropriate level of peer review to ensure that the information is scientifically credible, technically accurate, appropriately written for the intended audience, and designed and published in a professional manner.

This report received informal peer review by subject-matter experts who were not directly involved in the collection, analysis, or reporting of the data.

Data in this report were collected and analyzed using methods based on established, peer-reviewed protocols and were analyzed and interpreted within the guidelines of the protocols.

Views, statements, findings, conclusions, recommendations, and data in this report do not necessarily reflect views and policies of the National Park Service, U.S. Department of the Interior. Mention of trade names or commercial products does not constitute endorsement or recommendation for use by the U.S. Government.

This report is available from (http://science.nature.nps.gov/im/units/secn) and the Natural Resource Publications Management website (http://www.nature.nps.gov/publications/nrpm/).

Please cite this publication as:

Byrne, M. W., S. L. Corbett, and J. C. DeVivo. 2012. Vegetation community monitoring at Moores Creek National Battlefield, 2010. Natural Resource Data Series NPS/SECN/NRDS—2012/XXX. National Park Service, Fort Collins, Colorado.

NPS 324/112889, February 2012

Contents

Figures

Tables

List of Terms

Absolute cover: The total amount of ground surface that is covered by each species or group. Describes the amount of cover that each species or group represents in a stratum. Expressed as a percentage. Can exceed 100% due to overlap. The total cover of each species or group divided by the total possible cover for a plot.

Canopy species: Woody species known to occur in the midstory or overstory of the canopy, or shrub species that grow greater than or equal to 4 cm DBH and measureable at breast height (1.4 m).

Canopy stratum: The structural zone above 1.1 m (i.e., elbow height of a typical observer as per densiometer instructions) and consists of all live and dead plant material that affects the amount of light penetrating to the ground. This includes individual elements whose cover is also potentially measured and accounted for in the shrub- or groundcover-stratum measurements, but exceeds 1.1 m in height, is detected by the densiometer, and contributes to canopy cover. Also referred to as the midstory, overstory, or sub-canopy.

Cover: The vertical projection of the outermost extent of a species, or the extent of the shadow cast by the species if the sun were directly overhead. Foliar cover.

DBH: Diameter at breast height, or 1.4 m above the ground's surface.

Frequency: The number of times a species or group is detected in a plot, expressed as a percentage. Provides information on regularity at which a species or group is encountered.

Groundcover stratum: The structural zone that consists of all non-woody species (i.e., forbs and graminoids), and all woody species (i.e., shrubs and trees) with a DBH of less than 1 cm and seedlings 30 cm or less in height.

Relative cover: The cover of each species or group as a function of all other plant species that occurred in a plot. Describes the percentage of cover that each species represents out of the total vegetative cover in a stratum. Expressed as a percentage. Always sums to 100%. The total cover of each species or group divided by the sum of the cover of all other species that occur in a plot.

Seedlings: Woody dicotyledonous plants less than 30 cm in height.

Shrub stratum: All woody species greater than 30 cm in height with a DBH of 1–4 cm.

Stratum: A structural size category of vegetation at a site. These are the canopy, shrub, and groundcover layers.

Executive Summary

In 2009, the National Park Service (NPS) Southeast Coast Network (SECN) Inventory and Monitoring Network began collecting vegetation community data as part the NPS Vital Signs monitoring program. Information collected under this Vital Sign will be used to help managers make better informed decisions by understanding trends and variability related to plant species, frequency of occurrence, percent cover, diversity, and distribution in the groundcover, shrub, and canopy strata.

Within each stratum, vegetation communities were sampled using a hybrid of methods used by the North Carolina Vegetation Survey nested-subplot design (Peet et al. 1998) within a circular plot similar to the Forest Inventory and Analysis protocol (Bechtold and Patterson 2005). This report summarizes vegetation community data collected at Moores Creek National Battlefield in 2010.

1. Data were collected at seven spatially-balanced random locations at the Battlefield. The findings below apply only to portions of the park that meet the following site selection criteria:

    a) Sites are located within park boundaries and ownership.

    b) Sites must be sampleable within safety guidelines.

    c) Sites cannot be located in wholly non-natural areas, open water, or areas where application of the methods is inappropriate (such as marshes).

2. Sampling activities occurred at the Battlefield from 7/10/2010 to 7/12/2010.

3. Monitoring efforts resulted in the addition of 13 species, subspecies, or varieties to the park's species list.

4. Absolute canopy cover across the park was approximately 69%.

5. Pond cypress (*Taxodium ascendens*) had the largest average diameter at breast height of any canopy species at the park.

6. Fetterbush (*Lyonia lucida*) had the highest frequency of seedling occurrence, where the species occurred at two or more sites.

7. Sweetgum (*Liquidambar styraciflua*) was the most frequently occurring species in the shrub stratum.

8. Waxmyrtle (*Morella cerifera*) had the highest absolute and relative cover in the shrub stratum.

9. Greenbriar (*Smilax* sp.), yellow jessamine (*Gelsemium sempervirens*), and red maple (*Acer rubrum*) were the most frequently occurring species in the groundcover stratum.

10. Centipedegrass (*Eremochloa ophuroides*) dominated mowed lawn areas. Greenbriar (*Smilax* sp.) had the highest absolute and relative cover in the groundcover stratum in areas that were not mowed lawn.

11. The full dataset, and associated metadata, can be acquired from the data store at http://science.nature.nps.gov/nrdata/

Introduction

Overview

Vegetation communities provide many ecosystem services. Among their many functions, they are an important component of food webs and wildlife habitat for many species, and serve as a carbon sink, produce oxygen, cycle nutrients and energy through an ecosystem, influence the local climate, improve water quality, and moderate flooding and erosion. Plant communities also respond to multiple stressors such as changes in air quality, hydrology, disturbance regimes, and climate. Determining trends in vegetation communities is vital to understanding the ecological processes occurring at a site, and identifying stressors and their impacts.

Vegetation communities are dynamic entities with constant changes in composition, cover, distribution, and structure that reflect stressor response, natural or anthropogenic in origin. Disturbance is the primary stressor and regulating mechanism of SECN vegetation communities. The timing, type, and extent of the disturbance generally evokes a distinguishable response in the species composition, diversity, and structure of the landscape (Foster et al. 1998, Turner et al. 1990). The primary natural-disturbance processes in SECN parks are fire and weather (e.g., hurricanes, drought). Anthropogenic influences include fire suppression, landscape fragmentation, altered hydrology, and non-native species introduction.

The SECN is composed of a diverse assemblage of vegetation communities. Approximately 180 vegetation associations (i.e., fine-resolution floristic description), as defined by the National Vegetation and Classification System (FGDC 2008), occur in the SECN. These communities vary widely in distribution, species composition, and structure, and include sparsely vegetated primary dune communities, late successional old-growth bottomland hardwood forest communities, and highly diverse herbaceous-dominated mesic pine savannah communities.

Given the widespread anthropogenic influences in SECN parks and the importance of vegetation communities, quantifying trends in plant cover, frequency, diversity, and distribution is a high priority (DeVivo et al. 2008). Evaluating trends in these metrics provides measures for assessing the ecological integrity and sustainability of southeastern ecosystems, and identifying the need for specific management activities on our park lands. The National Park Service Omnibus Management Act of 1998, and other reinforcing policies and regulations, require park managers "to establish baseline information and to provide information on the long-term trends in the condition of National Park System resources" (Title II, Sec. 204). The vegetation-community monitoring data summarized herein is a tool to assist park managers in fulfilling this mandate.

This report summarizes data collected as a part of the SECN's Vegetation Community Vital Signs monitoring efforts.

Monitoring Objective

- Determine trends in plant species frequency, percent cover, diversity, and distribution in the groundcover, shrub, and canopy strata.

Methods

Study Area

Moores Creek National Battlefield (MOCR) is in southern-coastal North Carolina approximately 32 km (20 miles) northwest of Wilmington, NC (Figure 1). The Battlefield's primary purpose is to interpret the pivotal Revolutionary War battle that occurred on the site; however, the park hosts a variety of natural resources as well. The 36-ha (88-ac) park contains a small portion of Moores Creek in the western part of the park, just north of the confluence of Moores Creek with the Black River. Moores Creek is a tidally-influenced blackwater stream with an approximate width of 8 m (26 ft). Vegetation communities of the park include riparian areas, dry pine forests, and wet pine savannahs. The riparian areas are generally dominated by bald cypress (*Taxodium distichum*) while the uplands are a mix of loblolly pine (*Pinus taeda*) and sweetgum (*Liquidambar styraciflua*). A large area in the center of the park is in a restoration process to return it to its historic condition of wet savannah. Despite its small size, the park hosts several state-listed plant species, including flowering goldenrod (*Solidago verna*) (species of special concern), Carolina bogmint (*Macbridea caroliniana*) (state endangered), and Carolina grass of Parnassus (*Parnassia caroliniana*) (state threatened). Non-native plants that pose the greatest potential risk to the integrity of the plant communities at MOCR are Chinese privet (*Ligustrum sinense*), Chinese wisteria (*Wisteria sinensis*), and kudzu (*Pueraria lobata*).

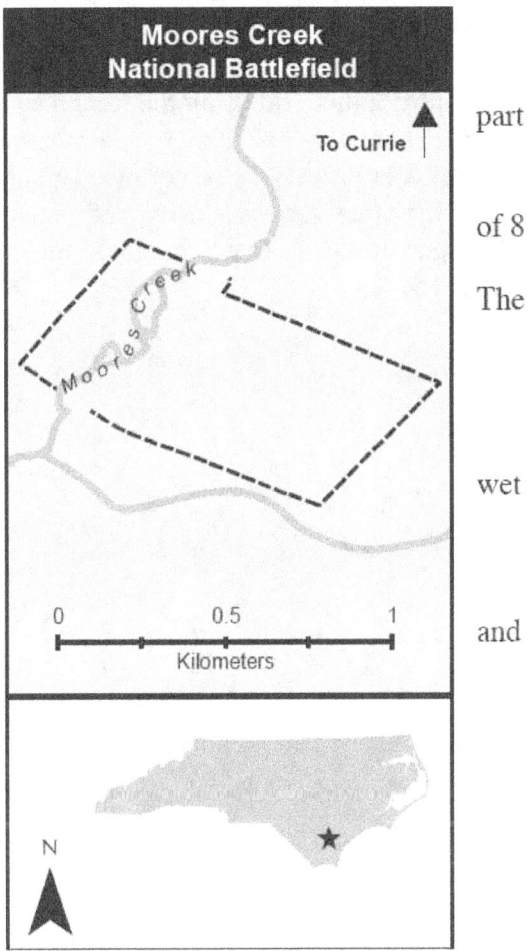

Figure 1. Location of Moores Creek National Battlefield.

A variety of previous land uses have affected the landscape and flora of MOCR. Formerly, a highway traversed the park, and this area has been slow to re-vegetate. Additionally, previous landowners cut several strait ditches and drains to alter the hydrology over much of the park. The park also has a history of timber production, which has dramatically altered the landscape by converting previous stands of longleaf pine (*Pinus palustris*) to loblolly pine (*Pinus taeda*). Although this area once contained forested swamps, the U.S. War Department burned many of them in the early part of the 20th century to improve the sites utility for military purposes. Despite a long extensive history of anthropogenic alterations, no known major forest diseases, pests, or introduced macrofauna currently have a substantial effect on the park. The area adjacent to the park consists of pulp-wood forests and other agriculture, although no established influence to park resources from these land use activities exists.

MOCR has 752 known vascular-plant species, subspecies, and varieties (NPSpecies 2011), including 13 species, subspecies, and varieties added to the species based on these monitoring efforts (Appendix A, Table 2).

Sampling Design

To allow for park-wide inference, the park's administrative boundary was used as the sampling frame, which was divided into a systematic 0.5-ha grid; the center point of each grid cell served as the potential sampling site and the grid cell served as the macroplot. A spatially-balanced sample was drawn from this grid using the Reversed Randomized Quadrant-Recursive Raster (RRQRR) algorithm (Theobald et al. 2007). Alternate points were used when selection criteria (i.e., including safety and access issues) were not met. A sample size of seven was chosen after consideration of park size, hypothesized variability, and logistical issues regarding travel time and conducting monitoring activities in five to six park units per year. Sampling at MOCR occurred from 7/10/2010 to 7/12/2010.

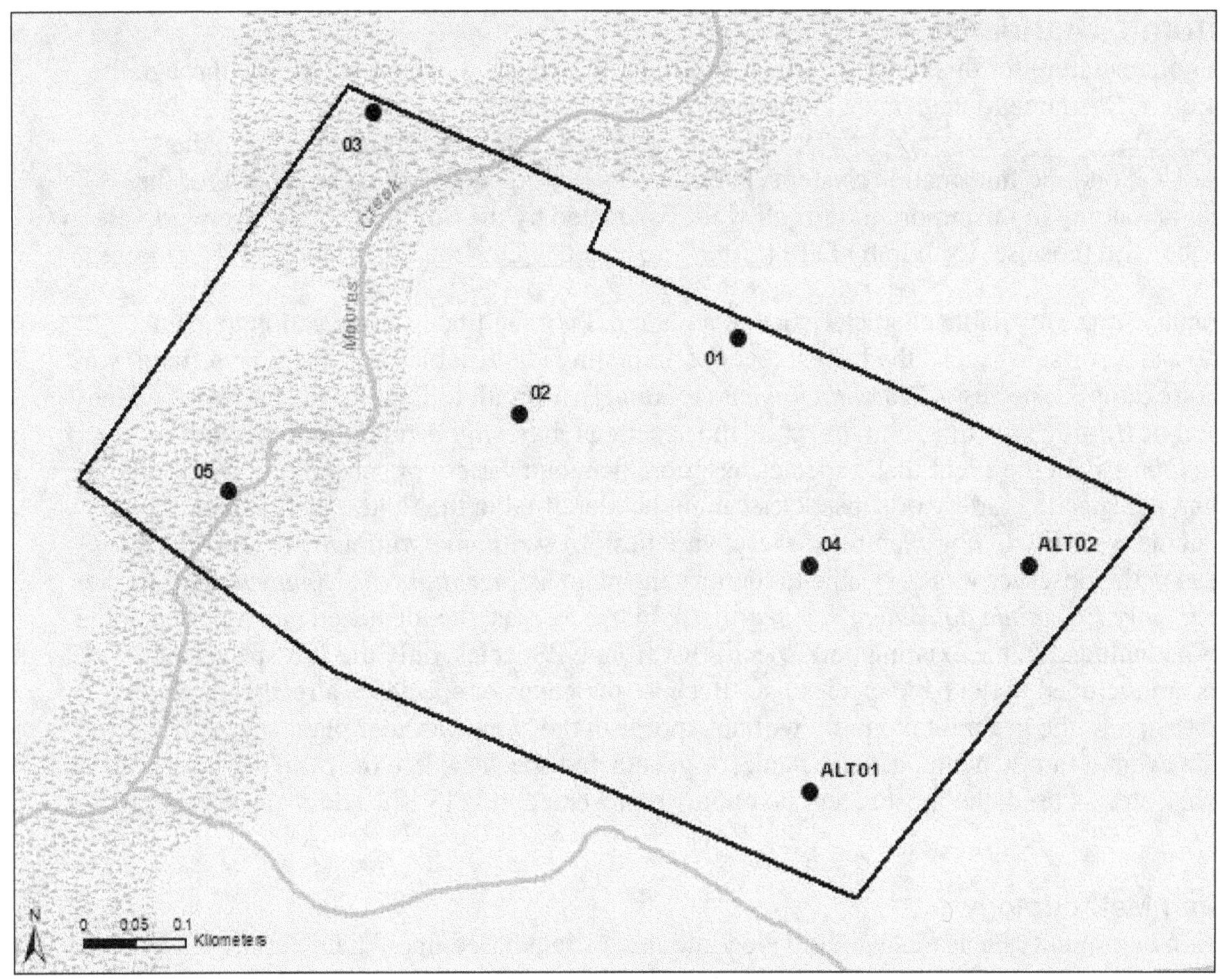

Figure 2. Spatially balanced random sampling locations at Moores Creek National Battlefield, 2010.

Taxonomic Standards

Species nomenclature for this report follow the current NPSpecies database accessible through the Integration of Resource Management Applications (IRMA) portal (https://irma.nps.gov/App/Portal/Home), which represents the most recent updates from the Integrated Taxonomic Information System (ITIS; http://www.itis.gov). Standards used for the botanical taxonomy in this report and for all work conducted by the Southeast Coast Network are in accordance with those set forth in by ITIS (http://irma.nps.gov/content/help/taxonomy/FAQ.aspx).

Occasionally, if the available characteristics of a plant did not facilitate identification to genus, species, variety, or subspecies, the lowest level of taxonomy identifiable (i.e., the most refined) was used. For example, species of *Dicanthelium* are extremely difficult to identify to species when they lack floral or fruiting structures. In this case, the specimen may only be identified to genus as *Dicanthelium* sp. In the event that a species has more than one variety or subspecies that occurs for a park and the specific variety or subspecies cannot be identified in the field, only the genus and species name were used. For example, several varieties of *Pteridium aquilinum* are known. If for some reason the observer was only able to identify the plant as *Pteridium aquilinum* and not further to variety, only *Pteridium aquilinum* was reported. In these cases, the identified and reported name may not be included in the existing park species list from NPSpecies, only the sub-species or varieties are included in the park species list. Because the genus or species is already known to occur in the park, the general taxonomy will not appear in the "new vascular plant species" (Table 2). In the event a family name, generic name, or genera and species name only (no variety, subspecies, etc.) is used, the most recent taxonomy represented in ITIS is used for these general terms.

Sampling Methodology

Vegetation community measures were divided into three strata based upon diameter at breast height (DBH) of woody species: canopy, shrub, and groundcover. Any non-woody (i.e., herbaceous) species was considered part of the groundcover stratum. Within each stratum, vegetation communities were sampled using a hybrid of methods used by the North Carolina Vegetation Survey nested-subplot design (Peet et al. 1998) within a circular plot similar to the Forest Inventory and Analysis protocol (Bechtold and Patterson 2005).

Plot Layout

The layout consisted of a circular plot with a radius of 15 m within the 0.5-ha macroplot. Subplots were systematically placed along six transects that radiated out from the center point at azimuths of 0°/360°, 60°, 120°, 180°, 240°, and 300° (Figure 3). To avoid overlap, subplots originated four meters from the macroplot (i.e., 0.5-ha grid) center point and extended away from the center point. Five measures were collected in the nested subplots within each plot: canopy cover, shrub cover, DBH, canopy-species seedling frequency, and herbaceous cover. Canopy cover was measured from the center point of the 0.5-ha macroplot. Shrub coverage was measured in two 2 × 4 m shrub plots along each transect. The shrub plots were further subdivided into 2 × 2 m subplots to improve cover-estimation accuracy and precision because cover-estimation error increases with plot size (solid gray shading, Figure 3). Groundcover coverage, groundcover nested frequency, and seedling frequency was measured in two 1 × 1 m groundcover plots (solid black shading, Figure 3) along each transect. Canopy species DBH was measured in three sections, each representing 1/3 of the total circular plot (hashed gray shading, Figure 3). A comprehensive species list was also compiled for all species occurring in the 0.5-ha macroplot. This macroplot list supplemented the list of species detected within the vegetation-community sampling plot (i.e., in the canopy, shrub, and groundcover plots).

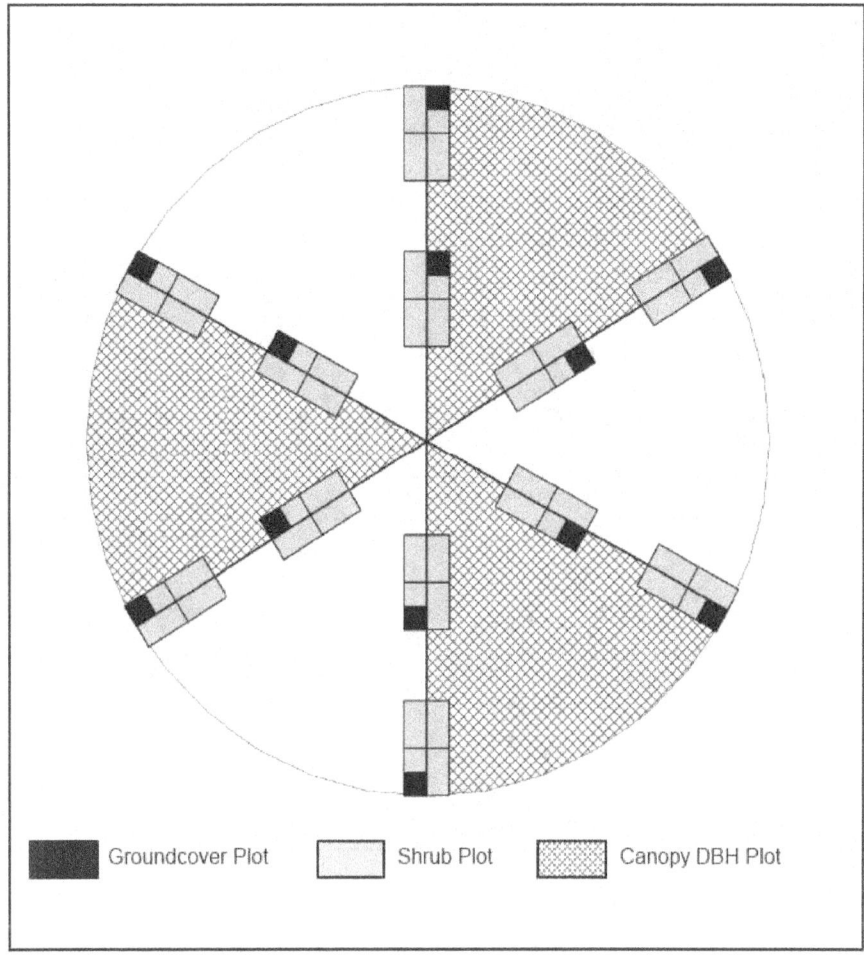

Figure 3. Southeast Coast Network vegetation-community monitoring plot layout.

Canopy Measures
Absolute canopy cover was estimated in the four cardinal directions with a concave spherical densiometer placed on a 1.1-m tall tripod at the plot center. Canopy cover reported is the mean of three observers across the four cardinal directions. The circular plot was subdivided into six sections occurring between the 0–60°, 120–180°, and 240–300° compass transects of the circular plot. Diameter at breast height (i.e., 1.37 m above the ground) was measured to the nearest millimeter for all trees (identified by species) with a diameter greater than or equal to 4 cm that occur within the 0–60°, 120–180°, and 240–300° section.

Shrub Measures
Shrub cover of all shrub species was visually estimated for each of the twelve 2 × 4 m plots. A common source of error in visual estimation of vegetation cover is that as plot size increases, cover-estimation error increases. Each shrub plot was therefore sub-divided into two 2 × 2 m subplots. The plots are situated at 15 m and 8 m (extending toward the plot center) along each of the transect lines of the circular plot. Shrub cover was categorized into one of seven coverage classes (Table 1) for each subplot. A coverage class of zero (Table 1) is assumed for any shrub species not detected

---

and not recorded on the datasheet. The measurements of subplots were combined by averaging the midpoint for the coverage class in the two shrub subplots resulting in a total shrub cover estimate for the 2 × 4 m plot. The authors have established consistent performance in the accuracy and precision of visual-cover estimates within and across observers in plots this size.

Groundcover Measures
Groundcover was visually estimated in each of the twelve 1 × 1 m plots situated on the clockwise side at 15 m and 8 m (extending toward the plot center) along each of the transect lines of the circular plot. Groundcover was categorized into one of seven coverage classes (Table 1) for each plot. A coverage class of zero (Table 1) is assumed for any groundcover species not detected and not recorded on the datasheet. The authors have established through trials that these coverage classes are discriminatory and repeatable across observers. Canopy-species seedling counts were estimated by counting the number of seedlings that occur in each of the 1 × 1 m plots.

Table 1. Cover estimation coverage class, percent cover range, and value used for analyses for SECN vegetation-community monitoring protocol.

Coverage Class	Percent Cover Range	Value Used for Analyses
0	0%	0.0
1	Trace (<1%)	0.5
2	1-5%	2.5
3	5-25%	15.0
4	25-50%	37.5
5	50-75%	62.5
6	75-95%	85.0
7	95-100%	97.5

Data Analysis
Because this is the first year of this protocol's implementation at the Battlefield, only the status of the elements presented in the aforementioned monitoring objective are determined; except diversity and distribution. The data in this report are presented by plot and pooled across plots. Sampling locations are presented in Figure 2 and summaries by plot are presented in Tables 3–9.

Summaries include (a) new species detected (Table 2), (b) canopy cover (Table 3), (c) canopy species size (Table 4), (d) seedling frequency (Table 5), (e) shrub species relative cover and frequency (Table 6), shrub species absolute cover and frequency (Table 7), (f) groundcover relative cover and frequency (Table 8), (g) groundcover absolute cover and frequency (Table 9), (h) species detected (Appendix A), and (i) species composition within and across macroplots (Appendix B).

Findings

We detected 107 species, subspecies, and varieties during this monitoring effort (Appendix A), including 13 new species, subspecies, and varieties not previously known to occur at the Battlefield (Table 2).

Table 2. New vascular plant species detected at Moores Creek National Battlefield during 2010 monitoring efforts and recommended NPSpecies classifications.

Species	Abundance	Nativity	Pest	Management Priority	Exploitation Concerns
Aralia spinosa	Unknown	Native	No	No	No
Conyza canadensis	Unknown	Native	No	No	No
Fraxinus pennsylvanica	Unknown	Native	No	No	No
Galactia elliottii	Unknown	Native	No	No	No
Galium aparine	Unknown	Native	No	No	No
Gaylussacia frondosa	Unknown	Native	No	No	No
Hydrocotyle umbellata	Unknown	Native	No	No	No
Ilex ambigua	Unknown	Native	No	No	No
Ilex vomitoria	Unknown	Native	No	No	No
Oxalis corniculata	Unknown	Native	No	No	No
Persea borbonia	Unknown	Native	No	No	No
Rhexia virginica	Unknown	Native	No	No	No
Rubus argutus	Unknown	Native	No	No	No

Measures of Community Structure

Absolute canopy cover was variable across the all sampling locations at the park ($\bar{x}$ = 68.87%, SD = 20.92; Table 3). The largest individual tree detected was a loblolly pine (*Pinus taeda*; 65.70 cm). Pond cypress (*Taxodium ascendens*) had the largest average DBH ($\bar{x}$ = 36.57 cm, SD = 14.3) of any species where ten or more individuals were sampled (Table 4). No longleaf pine (*Pinus palustris*) seedlings were detected, while loblolly pine seedlings were detected at a frequency of $0.31/m^2$ (Table 5). The most frequently detected seedling occurring at two or more sampling sites was fetterbush (*Lyonia lucida*) (frequency of $1.94/m^2$). Sweetgum (*Liquidambar styraciflua*) was the most frequently occurring shrub species at the park (f = 85.71), however waxmyrtle (*Morella cerifera*) had the highest relative cover in the park ($\bar{x}$ = 22.24%, SD =31.42; Table 6). Waxmyrtle also had the highest absolute cover in the shrub stratum at the park ($\bar{x}$ = 9.67%, SD = 16.19; Table 7). No non-native or invasive species were detected in the canopy or shrub strata. Greenbriar (*Smilax* sp.), yellow jessamine (*Gelsemium sempervirens*), and red maple (*Acer rubrum*) were the most frequently occurring species (85.71%, 71.43%, and 57.14% respectively) in the groundcover stratum (Table 8). Greenbriar (*Smilax* sp.) had the highest absolute cover in the groundcover stratum ($\bar{x}$ = 6.61%, SD = 5.91; Table 8). Centipedegrass (*Eremochloa ophuroides*) had the highest relative cover in the groundcover stratum ($\bar{x}$, = 10.21%, SD = 24.79) followed by *Smilax* sp. ($\bar{x}$ = 8.81%, SD = 8.65; Table 9). Centipedegrass only occurred at two sites, one of which was a mowed, maintained area adjacent to the park entry road, where *Smilax* sp. occurred at five of the six surveyed sites (Table 8, 9).

Table 3. Average canopy cover in vegetation monitoring sampling locations at Moores Creek National Battlefield, 2010.

Sampling Location	Average Canopy Cover	Standard Deviation
MOCR-1	70.75	6.22
MOCR-2	86	1.56
MOCR-3	88.83	2.52
MOCR-4	29.5	2.75
MOCR-5	81.25	5.81
MOCR-A1	54.08	4.56
MOCR-A2	71.67	1.44
Park Average	**68.87**	**20.92**

Table 4. Average canopy species size, measured as diameter (cm) at breast height (DBH) for species sampled in vegetation monitoring sampling locations at Moores Creek National Battlefield, 2010. Numbers in parentheses indicate the number of individual trees measured within each plot.

Species	Average	Standard Deviation	Sampling Point						
			1	2	3	4	5	A1	A2
Acer rubrum	16.40	13.00	11.78 (4)		20 00 (1)		15.13 (18)		28.93 (3)
Carya alba	14.65	2.76	14.65 (2)						
Cornus florida	8.16	3.71	8.16 (5)						
Cyrilla racemiflora	6.43	1.87			6.63 (10)		5.40 (2)		
Fraxinus caroliniana	6 04	1.22			6.21 (7)		5.73 (4)		
Ilex glabra	5 60		5.60 (1)						
Ilex opaca	10.66	4.74	13.93 (3)	7.70 (4)	12.70 (2)		8.60 (1)		
Liquidambar styraciflua	15.38	12.59	13.00 (6)	10 60 (13)	7.20 (1)	25.80 (1)	42 35 (4)		11.16 (8)
Morella cerifera	6.77	2.15	7.00 (2)	5 30 (1)					6 87 (10)
Nyssa biflora	18.31	12.50			25.12 (5)		9.80 (4)		
Nyssa sylvatica	8 20	5.09	11.80 (1)	4 60 (1)					
Persea palustris	15.60						15 60 (1)		
Pinus taeda	33.48	22.80	48.60 (4)	19.79 (20)	65.70 (1)	37.10 (1)		32.44 (9)	64.63 (6)
Prunus serotina var. serotina	10.80								10.80 (1)
Quercus falcata	7 20		7.20 (1)						
Quercus laurifolia	20.08	20.19	5.10 (1)		6.10 (2)		28 66 (5)		
Quercus lyrata	19.6						19 60 (1)		
Quercus nigra	12.08	8.45	18.60 (2)						5.55 (2)
Quercus stellata	19.4		19.40 (1)						
Salix caroliniana	13.3								13.30 (1)
Taxodium ascendens	36.57	14 3			58 80 (1)		34.10 (9)		
Vaccinium arboreum	7.6	1.13		7 60 (2)					
Acer rubrum (dead)	11.5	4.24	11.50 (2)						
Quercus laurifolia (dead)	49.05	0.07			49 05 (2)				
Quercus sp. (dead)	64.07	20.62		52.65 (2)					86.90 (1)
Unidentified Dead									
Magnoliopsida	21.95	15.34			32 80 (1)		11.10 (1)		

Table 5. Seedling frequency for canopy and shrub species in vegetation monitoring sampling locations at Moores Creek National Battlefield, 2010.

Species	Total Seedlings	Seedlings/m²	Std Dev	Sampling Point						
				1	2	3	4	5	A1	A2
Acer rubrum	94	1.12	1.94	0.17		2.50		5.00		0.17
Clethra alnifolia	94	1.12	2.68	0.67					7.17	
Cyrilla racemiflora	3	0 04	0.09					0.25		
Fraxinus caroliniana	6	0 07	0.12			0.25		0.25		
Gaylussacia dumosa	10	0.12	0.31	0.83						
Gaylussacia frondosa	4	0 05	0.13						0 33	
Ilex coriacea	1	0 01	0.03	0.08						
Ilex glabra	30	0 36	0.75	0.50					2 00	
Ilex opaca	2	0 02	0.04	0.08	0 08					
Ilex sp.	1	0 01	0.03					0.08		
Itea virginica	12	0.14	0.38					1.00		
Leucothoe racemosa	2	0 02	0.06	0.17						
Liquidambar styraciflua	29	0 35	0.78			0.33		2.08		
Lyonia lucida	163	1 94	5.06	0.17					13.42	
Morella cerifera	22	0 26	0.62				0.17			1 67
Nyssa biflora	63	0.75	1.77			0.50		4.75		
Nyssa sylvatica	5	0 06	0.1	0.17					0 25	
Persea borbonia	2	0 02	0.06	0.17						
Photinia pyrifolia	20	0 24	0.63						1 67	
Pinus taeda	26	0 31	0.35		0 08	0.42	0 33	0.33	1 00	
Quercus laurifolia	8	0.1	0.12			0.25		0.17		0 25
Quercus lyrata	1	0 01	0.03					0.08		
Quercus nigra	6	0 07	0.12	0.25	0 25					
Symplocos tinctoria	36	0.43	0.79	1.00					2 00	
Taxodium ascendens	1	0 01	0.03					0.08		
Vaccinium corymbosum	7	0 08	0.19	0.08					0 50	
Vaccinium crassifolium	171	2 04	5.39						14.25	
Vaccinium sp.	3	0 04	0.09			0.25				

Table 6. Percent of vegetation cover (relative cover) and frequency of occurrence of shrub species in vegetation monitoring sampling locations at Moores Creek National Battlefield, 2010.

Species	Frequency	Average	Standard Deviation	Sampling Point						
				1	2	3	4	5	A1	A2
Acer rubrum	57.14	6.48	12.71	9.52	1 23			34.23	0.42	
Carpinus caroliniana	14 29	2.1	5 56			14.71				
Carya alba	14 29	0.02	0 06	0.16						
Catalpa speciosa	14 29	0.28	0.75							1 99
Clethra alnifolia	28 57	3.13	5.47	8.86					13 02	
Cornus florida	14 29	0.49	1.3	3.45						
Cyrilla racemiflora	28 57	0.95	2 34					6 25	0.42	
Diospyros virginiana	14 29	0.15	0.4		1 05					
Fraxinus caroliniana	28 57	13.38	23.87			58.82		34.82		
Gaylussacia dumosa	28 57	0.97	2.14	5.75	1 05					
Gaylussacia frondosa	14 29	0.18	0.47						1.25	
Ilex ambigua	14 29	0.33	0 86		2 28					
Ilex coriacea	14 29	0.3	0 81	2.13						
Ilex glabra	42 86	5.42	8 25	5.42	11.03				21 52	
Ilex opaca	57.14	2.39	4 36	2.13	12.08		0.70	1.79		
Ilex sp.	14 29	0.3	0.79					2 08		
Itea virginica	14 29	0.68	1.8					4.76		
Leucothoe racemosa	14 29	0.28	0.74	1.97						
Liquidambar styraciflua	85.71	5.87	5.77	0.98	13.66	1.96	4.20		6.55	13.74
Lyonia lucida	28 57	4.31	10.91	1.15					29 03	
Magnolia grandiflora	42 86	0.44	0 55		1 05				1.04	0 99
Magnolia virginiana	14 29	0.33	0 86		2 28					
Morella cerifera	71.43	22.24	31.42	6.07	14.18		62 94		0.49	72.02
Nyssa sylvatica	42 86	1.66	2 26		5 25		4.20		2.16	
Persea borbonia	57.14	2.39	2 84	6.93	1 05				3.62	5.13
Photinia pyrifolia	28 57	0.89	1 56		3 68				2.58	
Pinus taeda	57.14	4.34	7 01	3.61	2.10		19 58		5.08	
Prunus serotina var. serotina	14 29	0.15	0.4		1 05					
Prunus sp.	14 29	0.15	0.4		1 05					
Quercus falcata	14 29	0.28	0.74	1.97						
Quercus laurifolia	71.43	5.97	6.73	19.53	3.15	6.86	4.20	8 04		
Quercus lyrata	14 29	0.89	2 36					6 25		
Quercus nigra	71.43	4.96	6 38	7.39	18.21		4.20		2.92	1 99
Salix caroliniana	14 29	0.14	0 38							0 99
Sassafras albidum	57.14	0.46	0 57	0.98	1 05				0.01	1.16
Symplocos tinctoria	57.14	2.33	3 68	8.54	0 04				6.75	0 99
Vaccinium arboreum	28 57	0.29	0.5	0.98	1 05					
Vaccinium corymbosum	57.14	1.12	1.17	2.46				1.79	2.58	0 99
Vaccinium crassifolium	14 29	0.08	0 21						0.56	
Vaccinium elliottii	28 57	2.03	4 39			2.45	11.76			
Vaccinium sp.	14 29	0.84	2 22				5.88			

Table 7. Percent area covered (absolute cover) and frequency of occurrence of shrub species sampled in vegetation monitoring sampling locations at Moores Creek National Battlefield, 2010.

Species	Frequency	Average	Standard Deviation	Sampling Point						
				1	2	3	4	5	A1	A2
Acer rubrum	57.14	2.77	4.61	6.04	0.73			11 98	0 63	
Carpinus caroliniana	14.29	0 22	0.59			1.56				
Carya alba	14.29	0 01	0.04	0.10						
Catalpa speciosa	14.29	0.18	0.47							1.25
Clethra alnifolia	28.57	3 59	7.31	5.63					19.48	
Cornus florida	14.29	0 31	0.83	2.19						
Cyrilla racemiflora	28.57	0.4	0.82					2.19	0 63	
Diospyros virginiana	14.29	0 09	0.24		0 63					
Fraxinus caroliniana	28.57	2 63	4.81			6.25		12.19		
Gaylussacia dumosa	28.57	0 61	1.36	3.65	0 63					
Gaylussacia frondosa	14.29	0 27	0.71						1 88	
Ilex ambigua	14.29	0.19	0.51		1 35					
Ilex coriacea	14.29	0.19	0.51	1.35						
Ilex glabra	42.86	6 03	11.81	3.44	6 56				32.19	
Ilex opaca	57.14	1 32	2.63	1.35	7.19		0.10	0.63		
Ilex sp.	14.29	0.1	0.28					0.73		
Itea virginica	14.29	0 24	0.63					1.67		
Leucothoe racemosa	14.29	0.18	0.47	1.25						
Liquidambar styraciflua	85.71	4	4.57	0.63	8.13	0.21	0 63		9.79	8.65
Lyonia lucida	28.57	6 31	16.37	0.73					43.44	
Magnolia grandiflora	42.86	0.4	0.59		0 63				1 56	0.63
Magnolia virginiana	14.29	0.19	0.51		1 35					
Morella cerifera	71.43	9 67	16.19	3.85	8.44		9 38		0.73	45.31
Nyssa sylvatica	42.86	1	1.51		3.13		0 63		3 23	
Persea borbonia	57.14	1 95	2.34	4.40	0 63				5.42	3.23
Photinia pyrifolia	28.57	0 86	1.55		2.19				3 85	
Pinus taeda	57.14	2 01	2.74	2.29	1 25		2 92		7 60	
Prunus serotina var. serotina	14.29	0 09	0.24		0 63					
Prunus sp.	14.29	0 09	0.24		0 63					
Quercus falcata	14.29	0.18	0.47	1.25						
Quercus laurifolia	71.43	2 63	4.42	12.40	1 88	0.73	0 63	2.81		
Quercus lyrata	14.29	0 31	0.83					2.19		
Quercus nigra	71.43	3.11	3.93	4.69	10.83		0 63		4 38	1.25
Salix caroliniana	14.29	0 09	0.24							0.63
Sassafras albidum	57.14	0 29	0.35	0.63	0 63				0 02	0.73
Symplocos tinctoria	57.14	2 31	3.97	5.42	0 02				10.10	0.63
Vaccinium arboreum	28.57	0.18	0.3	0.63	0 63					
Vaccinium corymbosum	57.14	0 95	1.4	1.56				0.63	3 85	0.63
Vaccinium crassifolium	14.29	0.12	0.31						0 83	
Vaccinium elliottii	28.57	0 39	0.66		1.46	1.25				
Vaccinium sp.	14.29	0 09	0.24			0.63				

Table 8. Percent of vegetation cover (relative cover) and frequency of occurrence of groundcover species in vegetation monitoring sampling locations at Moores Creek National Battlefield, 2010.

Species	Frequency	Average	Standard Deviation	1	2	3	4	5	A1	A2
				\[Sampling Point\]						
Acalypha gracilens	14.29	0.11	0 3				0.8			
Acer rubrum	57.14	0.99	1.64	0.19		4.06		2.54		0.15
Aristida stricta	14.29	0.12	0.32						0.84	
Arundinaria gigantea	42.86	0.91	1.18		2.71			1.98	1.67	
Axonopus sp.	14.29	0.1	0.26				0 68			
Bignonia capreolata	28.57	0.04	0.08	0.19			0.11			
Campsis radicans	14.29	0.11	0 3					0.79		
Carex sp.	28.57	0.76	1.38			3.47		1.85		
Chamaesyce maculata	14.29	0.02	0.04				0.11			
Chasmanthium laxum	28.57	0.23	0.4					0.79	0.84	
Clethra alnifolia	28.57	0.99	1.81	2 33					4 6	
Conyza canadensis	14.29	0.02	0.04				0.11			
Cyperus sp.	14.29	0.02	0.04				0.11			
Cyrilla racemiflora	14.29	0.11	0 3					0.79		
Dichanthelium sp.	14.29	0.1	0.26				0 68			
Diodia teres	14.29	0.02	0.04				0.11			
Eremochloa ophiuroides	28.57	5.63	13 53		3.23		36.19			
Erigeron vernus	14.29	0.02	0.04				0.11			
Fraxinus caroliniana	28.57	0.3	0.7			1.87		0.26		
Gaylussacia dumosa	14.29	0.19	0.51	1 36						
Gaylussacia frondosa	14.29	0.14	0.37						0.98	
Gelsemium sempervirens	71.43	1.68	1.69		4.78		1 59	0.79	2.65	1 96
Hydrocotyle umbellata	14.29	0.04	0.1			0.27				
Hymenocallis floridana	14.29	0.11	0 3					0.79		
Hymenocallis sp.	14.29	0.04	0.1			0.27				
Hypericum hypericoides	14.29	0.23	0 6					1.58		
Hypericum sp.	14.29	0.02	0.05				0.14			
Hypoxis hirsuta var. leptocarpa	14.29	0.28	0.75					1.98		
Ilex coriacea	14.29	0.03	0.07	0.19						
Ilex glabra	28.57	0.49	0 9	1.17					2.29	
Ilex opaca	28.57	0.05	0.08	0.19	0.13					
Ilex sp.	14.29	0	0.01					0.03		
Itea virginica	14.29	0.15	0.4					1.06		
Leucothoe racemosa	14.29	0.03	0.07	0.19						
Liquidambar styraciflua	28.57	0.55	0.95			1.87		2.01		
Lyonia lucida	28.57	1.19	3.06	0.19					8.12	
Medicago sp.	14.29	0.1	0.26				0 68			
Mitchella repens	28.57	0.28	0.49	1.17				0.79		
Morella cerifera	28.57	0.45	1.14				0.11			3 02
Nyssa biflora	28.57	0.8	1.78			0 8		4.78		
Nyssa sylvatica	28.57	0.15	0.31	0.19					0.84	
Panicum sp.	42.86	0.54	0.97	1.17				2.51	0.14	
Parthenocissus quinquefolia	42.86	0.84	1.11		1.55		1 59			2.72
Paspalum notatum	14.29	0.1	0.26				0 68			
Paspalum sp.	14.29	0.02	0.04				0.11			
Persea borbonia	14.29	0.17	0.44	1.17						
Photinia pyrifolia	14.29	0.36	0.95						2.51	
Pinus taeda	71.43	0.48	0.72		0.03	0.27	0 25	0.82	1.98	
Polypremum procumbens	14.29	0.2	0.52				1 37			
Potentilla canadensis	14.29	0.02	0.04				0.11			
Quercus laurifolia	42.86	0.1	0.13			0.27		0.26		0.18
Quercus lyrata	14.29	0.02	0.05					0.13		
Quercus nigra	28.57	0.09	0.16	0 39	0.26					
Quercus sp.	14.29	0	0.01				0 02			
Rubus argutus	14.29	0.03	0.09				0 23			
Scleria triglomerata	14.29	0.11	0 3					0.79		
Smilax rotundifolia	14.29	0.74	1.95		5.17					
Smilax sp.	85.71	6.61	5.91	4 08	10.98	7.75		5.55	0.98	16.91
Symplocos tinctoria	28.57	0.6	1.05	2 52					1.67	
Taxodium ascendens	14.29	0.02	0.05					0.13		

Table 8. Continued.

Species	Frequency	Average	Standard Deviation	Sampling Point						
				1	2	3	4	5	A1	A2
Toxicodendron radicans	57.14	0.49	0.82		2.2	0.27			0.03		0 91
Vaccinium corymbosum	28.57	0.21	0.47	0.19						1.26	
Vaccinium crassifolium	14.29	0.48	1.27							3.35	
Vaccinium sp.	14.29	0.23	0.61			1 6					
Vitis rotundifolia	42.86	2.27	3.15	4 85	7.88						3.17
Wisteria sinensis	14.29	0.33	0.88	2 33							
Woodwardia areolata	28.57	0.46	0.78			1 6		1.58		
Woodwardia virginica	14.29	0.4	1.05					2.77		
Unidentified										
Cyperaceae	14.29	0.02	0.05		0.13					
Lamiaceae	28.57	0.21	0.36		0.77		0 68			
Magnoliopsida	14.29	0.23	0.61			1 6				
Poaceae	28.57	0.13	0.26		0.26		0 68			
Ground Condition										
Aquatic or obligate non-vascular plants	28.57	2.8	5.72			15 23		4.36		
Bare Ground	42.86	0.74	1.22	2 52	0.13		2.5			
Exposed Rock	14.29	1.44	3.81		10.07					
Leaf Litter or Duff	100	58.48	6.96	63.69	49.73	58.79	50.08	55.47	65 29	66.29
Open Water	14.29	0.54	1.43							3.78
Tree Stump	28.57	0.24	0.42					0.79		0 91
Upland non-vascular plants or lichens	42.86	1.69	3.61	9.71			0.11	1.98		

Table 9. Percent area covered (absolute cover) and frequency of occurrence by groundcover species sampled in vegetation monitoring sampling locations at Moores Creek National Battlefield, 2010.

Species	Frequency	Average	Standard Deviation	Sampling Point						
				1	2	3	4	5	A1	A2
Acalypha gracilens	14.29	0.21	0 55				1.46			
Acer rubrum	57.14	1.08	1.73	0.21		3.17		4		0.21
Aristida stricta	14.29	0.18	0.47					1.25		
Arundinaria gigantea	42.86	1.43	1 87		4 38			3.13	2.5	
Axonopus sp.	14.29	0.18	0.47				1 25			
Bignonia capreolata	28.57	0.06	0.1	0.21			0 21			
Campsis radicans	14.29	0.18	0.47					1.25		
Carex sp.	28.57	0 8	1 37			2.71		2.92		
Chamaesyce maculata	14.29	0.03	0 08				0 21			
Chasmanthium laxum	28.57	0.36	0 61					1.25	1.25	
Clethra alnifolia	28.57	1.34	2 61	2.5					6.88	
Conyza canadensis	14.29	0.03	0 08				0 21			
Cyperus sp.	14.29	0.03	0 08				0 21			
Cyrilla racemiflora	14.29	0.18	0.47					1.25		
Dichanthelium sp.	14.29	0.18	0.47				1 25			
Diodia teres	14.29	0.03	0 08				0 21			
Eremochloa ophiuroides	28.57	10 21	24.79		5 21		66.25			
Erigeron vernus	14.29	0.03	0 08				0 21			
Fraxinus caroliniana	28.57	0.27	0 55			1.46		0.42		
Gaylussacia dumosa	14.29	0.21	0 55	1.46						
Gaylussacia frondosa	14.29	0.21	0 55						1.46	
Gelsemium sempervirens	71.43	2.65	2 69		7.71		2 92	1.25	3.96	2.71
Hydrocotyle umbellata	14.29	0.03	0 08		0 21					
Hymenocallis floridana	14.29	0.18	0.47					1.25		
Hymenocallis sp.	14.29	0.03	0 08		0 21					
Hypericum hypericoides	14.29	0.36	0 94					2.5		
Hypericum sp.	14.29	0.04	0 09				0 25			
Hypoxis hirsuta var. leptocarpa	14.29	0.45	1.18					3.13		
Ilex coriacea	14.29	0.03	0 08	0.21						
Ilex glabra	28.57	0.67	1.3	1.25					3.42	
Ilex opaca	28.57	0.06	0.1	0.21	0 21					
Ilex sp.	14.29	0.01	0 02					0.04		
Itea virginica	14.29	0.24	0 63					1.67		
Leucothoe racemosa	14.29	0.03	0 08	0.21						
Liquidambar styraciflua	28.57	0.66	1 23			1.46		3.17		
Lyonia lucida	28.57	1.76	4 57	0.21					12.13	
Medicago sp.	14.29	0.18	0.47				1 25			
Mitchella repens	28.57	0.36	0 61	1.25				1.25		
Morella cerifera	28.57	0.63	1 56				0 21			4.17
Nyssa biflora	28.57	1.17	2 82			0 63		7.54		
Nyssa sylvatica	28.57	0.21	0.47	0.21				1.25		
Panicum sp.	42.86	0.77	1.48	1.25				3.96	0.21	
Parthenocissus quinquefolia	42.86	1.31	1 67		2.5		2 92			3.75
Paspalum notatum	14.29	0.18	0.47				1 25			
Paspalum sp.	14.29	0.03	0 08				0 21			
Persea borbonia	14.29	0.18	0.47	1.25						
Photinia pyrifolia	14.29	0.54	1.42						3.75	
Pinus taeda	71.43	0.71	1 09		0 04	0 21	0.46	1.29	2.96	
Polypremum procumbens	14.29	0.36	0 94				2.5			
Potentilla canadensis	14.29	0.03	0 08				0 21			
Quercus laurifolia	42.86	0.13	0.17			0 21		0.42		0.25
Quercus lyrata	14.29	0.03	0 08					0.21		
Quercus nigra	28.57	0.12	0.2	0.42	0.42					
Quercus sp.	14.29	0.01	0 02				0 04			
Rubus argutus	14.29	0.06	0.16				0.42			
Scleria triglomerata	14.29	0.18	0.47					1.25		
Smilax rotundifolia	14.29	1.19	3.15		8 33					
Smilax sp.	85.71	8.81	8 65	4.38	17.71	6 04		8.75	1.46	23 33
Symplocos tinctoria	28.57	0.74	1 27	2.71					2.5	
Taxodium ascendens	14.29	0.03	0 08					0.21		

Table 9. Continued.

				Sampling Point						
Toxicodendron radicans	57.14	0.72	1 32		3 54	0 21		0.04		1.25
Vaccinium corymbosum	28.57	0 3	0.7	0.21					1.88	
Vaccinium crassifolium	14.29	0.71	1 89						5	
Vaccinium sp.	14.29	0.18	0 47			1 25				
Vitis rotundifolia	42.86	3.18	4.77	5.21	12.71					4.38
Wisteria sinensis	14.29	0.36	0 94	2.5						
Woodwardia areolata	28.57	0.54	0 98			1 25		2.5		
Woodwardia virginica	14.29	0.63	1 65					4.38		
Unidentified										
Cyperaceae	14.29	0.03	0 08		0 21					
Lamiaceae	28.57	0.36	0 61		1 25	1 25				
Magnoliopsida	14.29	0.18	0.47			1 25				
Poaceae	28.57	0.24	0.47		0.42	1 25				
Ground Condition										
Aquatic or obligate non-vascular plants	28.57	2.68	4.8			11.88		6.88		
Bare Ground	42.86	1.07	1 84	2.71	0 21		4 58			
Exposed Rock	14.29	2.32	6.14		16.25					
Leaf Litter or Duff	100	80 36	17.95	68.33	80.21	45.83	91.67	87.5	97.5	91.46
Open Water	14.29	0.74	1 97							5.21
Tree Stump	28.57	0.36	0 61					1.25		1.25
Upland non-vascular plants or lichens	42.86	1.96	3.9	10.42			0 21	3.13		

Literature Cited

Bechtold, W. A. and P. L. Patterson, (eds.). 2005. The enhanced forest inventory and analysis program — national sampling design and estimation procedures. General Technical Report SRS-80. USDA Forest Service, Southern Research Station, Asheville, NC. 85 pp.

Byrne, M. W. 2009. Sampling-point generation for SECN monitoring protocols: Generating a spatially-balanced random sample with the RRQRR tool in ArcGIS 9.1. Draft Standard Operating Procedure Version 1.0, last updated March 2009.

Byrne, M. W., S. L. Corbett, E. Thompson, and C. J. Wright. *In preparation*. Draft vegetation community monitoring in Southeast Coast Network parks. USDI National Park Service, Southeast Coast Network, Atlanta, GA, USA.

DeVivo, J. C., C. J. Wright, M. W. Byrne, E. DiDonato, and T. Curtis. 2008. Vital signs monitoring in the Southeast Coast Inventory & Monitoring Network. Natural Resource Report NPS/SECN/NRR—2008/061. USDI National Park Service, Fort Collins, CO, USA.

Federal Geographic Data Committee. 2008. National vegetation classification standard, version 2. FGDC-STD-005-2008. Available online: http://www.fgdc.gov/standards/project/FGDC-standards-projects/vegetation.

Foster, D. R., G. Motzkin, and B. Slater. 1998. Land-use history as long-term broad-scale disturbance: regional forest dynamics in central New England. Ecosystems: 1:96-119.

NPSpecies - The National Park Service Biodiversity Database. Secure online version. https://science1.nature.nps.gov/npspecies/web/main/start (Park list: accessed 1/13/2011).

Peet R. K., T. R. Wentworth, and P. S White. 1998. A flexible, multipurpose method for recording vegetation composition and structure. Castanea 63:262-274.

Theobald, D. M., D. L. Stevens, D. White, N. S. Urquhart, A. R. Olsen, and J. B. Norman. 2007. Using GIS to generate spatially balanced random survey designs for natural resource applications Environmental Management 40:134-146.

Turner, II, B. L., W. C. Clark, R. W. Kates, J. F. Richards, J. T. Mathews, and W. B. Meyer, (eds.). 1990. The earth as transformed by human action: Global and regional changes in the biosphere over the past 300 years. Cambridge University Press, Cambridge, UK.

Appendix A. Plant species known to occur at Moores Creek National Battlefield.

Table A-1. Vascular plant species known occur at Moores Creek National Battlefield (NPSpecies 2011) and species detected during 2010 monitoring efforts.

Order	Family	Species	NPSpecies	This Study
Scrophulariales	Acanthaceae	*Justicia ovata*	X	
Sapindales	Aceraceae	*Acer rubrum*	X	X
Sapindales	Aceraceae	*Acer saccharum ssp. floridanum*	X	
Liliales	Agavaceae	*Yucca filamentosa*	X	
Alismatales	Alismataceae	*Sagittaria graminea*	X	
Alismatales	Alismataceae	*Sagittaria subulata*	X	
Sapindales	Anacardiaceae	*Rhus copallina*		X
Sapindales	Anacardiaceae	*Rhus copallinum*	X	
Sapindales	Anacardiaceae	*Rhus glabra*	X	
Sapindales	Anacardiaceae	*Toxicodendron pubescens*	X	
Sapindales	Anacardiaceae	*Toxicodendron radicans*	X	X
Apiales	Apiaceae	*Centella asiatica*	X	
Apiales	Apiaceae	*Centella erecta*	X	
Apiales	Apiaceae	*Cicuta mexicana*	X	
Apiales	Apiaceae	*Eryngium integrifolium*	X	
Apiales	Apiaceae	*Hydrocotyle umbellata*		X
Apiales	Apiaceae	*Hydrocotyle verticillata var. verticillata*	X	
Apiales	Apiaceae	*Oxypolis rigidior*	X	
Apiales	Apiaceae	*Ptilimnium capillaceum*	X	
Apiales	Apiaceae	*Spermolepis divaricata*	X	
Gentianales	Apocynaceae	*Amsonia tabernaemontana*	X	
Gentianales	Apocynaceae	*Vinca angustifolia*	X	
Gentianales	Apocynaceae	*Vinca minor*	X	
Celastrales	Aquifoliaceae	*Ilex ambigua*		X
Celastrales	Aquifoliaceae	*Ilex amelanchier*	X	
Celastrales	Aquifoliaceae	*Ilex cassine var. myrtifolia*	X	
Celastrales	Aquifoliaceae	*Ilex coriacea*	X	X
Celastrales	Aquifoliaceae	*Ilex glabra*	X	X
Celastrales	Aquifoliaceae	*Ilex opaca*	X	X
Celastrales	Aquifoliaceae	*Ilex verticillata*	X	
Celastrales	Aquifoliaceae	*Ilex vomitoria*		X
Arales	Araceae	*Orontium aquaticum*	X	
Apiales	Araliaceae	*Aralia spinosa*		X
Arecales	Arecaceae	*Sabal minor*	X	
Aristolochiales	Aristolochiaceae	*Hexastylis arifolia*	X	X
Aristolochiales	Aristolochiaceae	*Hexastylis virginica*	X	
Gentianales	Asclepiadaceae	*Asclepias amplexicaulis*	X	
Gentianales	Asclepiadaceae	*Asclepias rubra*	X	
Gentianales	Asclepiadaceae	*Asclepias tuberosa*	X	
Polypodiales	Aspleniaceae	*Asplenium platyneuron*	X	X
Asterales	Asteraceae	*Achillea millefolium*	X	
Asterales	Asteraceae	*Ambrosia artemisiifolia*	X	X
Asterales	Asteraceae	*Antennaria plantaginifolia*	X	
Asterales	Asteraceae	*Anthemis arvensis*	X	
Asterales	Asteraceae	*Aster dumosus*	X	

Table A-1. Continued.

Order	Family	Species	NPSpecies	This Study
Asterales	Asteraceae	*Aster lateriflorus*	X	
Asterales	Asteraceae	*Aster novi-belgii*	X	
Asterales	Asteraceae	*Aster pilosus*	X	
Asterales	Asteraceae	*Aster pilosus var. pilosus*	X	
Asterales	Asteraceae	*Aster simplex*	X	
Asterales	Asteraceae	*Baccharis halimifolia*	X	
Asterales	Asteraceae	*Bidens aristosa*	X	
Asterales	Asteraceae	*Bidens bipinnata*	X	
Asterales	Asteraceae	*Bidens frondosa*	X	
Asterales	Asteraceae	*Bigelowia nudata*	X	
Asterales	Asteraceae	*Carduus spinosissimus*	X	
Asterales	Asteraceae	*Carphephorus bellidifolius*	X	
Asterales	Asteraceae	*Carphephorus paniculatus*	X	
Asterales	Asteraceae	*Carphephorus tomentosus*	X	
Asterales	Asteraceae	*Chaptalia tomentosa*	X	
Asterales	Asteraceae	*Chrysopsis gossypina ssp. gossypina*	X	
Asterales	Asteraceae	*Chrysopsis mariana*	X	
Asterales	Asteraceae	*Cirsium horridulum*	X	
Asterales	Asteraceae	*Cirsium repandum*	X	
Asterales	Asteraceae	*Cirsium virginianum*	X	
Asterales	Asteraceae	*Conoclinium coelestinum*	X	
Asterales	Asteraceae	*Conyza canadensis*		X
Asterales	Asteraceae	*Coreopsis falcata*	X	
Asterales	Asteraceae	*Coreopsis gladiata*	X	
Asterales	Asteraceae	*Coreopsis lanceolata*	X	
Asterales	Asteraceae	*Coreopsis leavenworthii*	X	
Asterales	Asteraceae	*Coreopsis linifolia*	X	
Asterales	Asteraceae	*Croptilon divaricatum*	X	
Asterales	Asteraceae	*Eclipta prostrata*	X	
Asterales	Asteraceae	*Elephantopus nudatus*	X	
Asterales	Asteraceae	*Elephantopus tomentosus*	X	
Asterales	Asteraceae	*Erechtites hieracifolia*	X	
Asterales	Asteraceae	*Erigeron canadensis var. canadensis*	X	
Asterales	Asteraceae	*Erigeron quercifolius*	X	
Asterales	Asteraceae	*Erigeron strigosus*	X	
Asterales	Asteraceae	*Erigeron vernus*	X	X
Asterales	Asteraceae	*Eupatorium anomalum*	X	
Asterales	Asteraceae	*Eupatorium aromaticum*	X	
Asterales	Asteraceae	*Eupatorium capillifolium*	X	X
Asterales	Asteraceae	*Eupatorium capillifolium var. capillifolium*	X	
Asterales	Asteraceae	*Eupatorium compositifolium*	X	
Asterales	Asteraceae	*Eupatorium dubium*	X	
Asterales	Asteraceae	*Eupatorium hyssopifolium*	X	
Asterales	Asteraceae	*Eupatorium leucolepis*	X	
Asterales	Asteraceae	*Eupatorium mohrii*	X	
Asterales	Asteraceae	*Eupatorium pilosum*	X	
Asterales	Asteraceae	*Eupatorium rotundifolium*	X	
Asterales	Asteraceae	*Eupatorium rotundifolium var. rotundifolium*	X	
Asterales	Asteraceae	*Eupatorium semiserratum*	X	
Asterales	Asteraceae	*Eurybia paludosa*	X	
Asterales	Asteraceae	*Euthamia tenuifolia*	X	

Table A-1. Continued.

Order	Family	Species	NPSpecies	This Study
Asterales	Asteraceae	*Gamochaeta purpurea*	X	
Asterales	Asteraceae	*Gnaphalium obtusifolium*	X	
Asterales	Asteraceae	*Gnaphalium purpureum var. purpureum*	X	
Asterales	Asteraceae	*Helenium amarum*	X	
Asterales	Asteraceae	*Helenium brevifolium*	X	
Asterales	Asteraceae	*Helenium flexuosum*	X	
Asterales	Asteraceae	*Helianthus angustifolius*	X	
Asterales	Asteraceae	*Helianthus atrorubens*	X	
Asterales	Asteraceae	*Helianthus heterophyllus*	X	
Asterales	Asteraceae	*Heterotheca gossypina*	X	
Asterales	Asteraceae	*Heterotheca nervosa*	X	
Asterales	Asteraceae	*Heterotheca nervosa var. nervosa*	X	
Asterales	Asteraceae	*Heterotheca subaxillaris*	X	
Asterales	Asteraceae	*Hieracium gronovii*	X	
Asterales	Asteraceae	*Hypochaeris radicata*	X	
Asterales	Asteraceae	*Ionactis linariifolius*	X	
Asterales	Asteraceae	*Krigia caespitosa*	X	
Asterales	Asteraceae	*Krigia dandelion*	X	
Asterales	Asteraceae	*Krigia virginica*	X	
Asterales	Asteraceae	*Lactuca canadensis*	X	
Asterales	Asteraceae	*Lactuca graminifolia*	X	
Asterales	Asteraceae	*Liatris graminifolia*	X	
Asterales	Asteraceae	*Liatris spicata*	X	
Asterales	Asteraceae	*Marshallia graminifolia*	X	
Asterales	Asteraceae	*Mikania scandens*	X	X
Asterales	Asteraceae	*Packera anonyma*	X	
Asterales	Asteraceae	*Packera tomentosa*	X	
Asterales	Asteraceae	*Pluchea camphorata*	X	
Asterales	Asteraceae	*Pluchea carolinensis*	X	
Asterales	Asteraceae	*Pluchea foetida*	X	
Asterales	Asteraceae	*Prenanthes altissima*	X	
Asterales	Asteraceae	*Prenanthes autumnalis*	X	
Asterales	Asteraceae	*Pterocaulon virgatum*	X	
Asterales	Asteraceae	*Pyrrhopappus carolinianus*	X	
Asterales	Asteraceae	*Sericocarpus asteroides*	X	
Asterales	Asteraceae	*Sericocarpus tortifolius*	X	
Asterales	Asteraceae	*Silphium compositum var. compositum*	X	
Asterales	Asteraceae	*Solidago altissima*	X	
Asterales	Asteraceae	*Solidago arguta*	X	
Asterales	Asteraceae	*Solidago fistulosa*	X	
Asterales	Asteraceae	*Solidago gracillima*	X	
Asterales	Asteraceae	*Solidago odora*	X	
Asterales	Asteraceae	*Solidago patula var. strictula*	X	
Asterales	Asteraceae	*Solidago petiolaris*	X	
Asterales	Asteraceae	*Solidago rugosa ssp. aspera*	X	
Asterales	Asteraceae	*Solidago rugosa var. rugosa*	X	
Asterales	Asteraceae	*Solidago stricta*	X	
Asterales	Asteraceae	*Solidago verna*	X	
Asterales	Asteraceae	*Sonchus asper*	X	
Asterales	Asteraceae	*Symphyotrichum dumosum var. dumosum*	X	
Asterales	Asteraceae	*Symphyotrichum pilosum var. pilosum*	X	

Table A-1. Continued.

Order	Family	Species	NPSpecies	This Study
Asterales	Asteraceae	*Symphyotrichum racemosum*	X	
Asterales	Asteraceae	*Symphyotrichum walteri*	X	
Asterales	Asteraceae	*Taraxacum officinale*	X	
Asterales	Asteraceae	*Vernonia angustifolia*	X	
Asterales	Asteraceae	*Xanthium strumarium var. glabratum*	X	
Ranunculales	Berberidaceae	*Mahonia aquifolium*	X	
Fagales	Betulaceae	*Alnus serrulata*	X	
Fagales	Betulaceae	*Betula nigra*	X	X
Fagales	Betulaceae	*Carpinus caroliniana*	X	X
Scrophulariales	Bignoniaceae	*Bignonia capreolata*	X	X
Scrophulariales	Bignoniaceae	*Campsis radicans*	X	X
Scrophulariales	Bignoniaceae	*Catalpa speciosa*	X	X
Polypodiales	Blechnaceae	*Woodwardia areolata*	X	X
Polypodiales	Blechnaceae	*Woodwardia virginica*	X	X
Capparales	Brassicaceae	*Arabidopsis thaliana*	X	
Capparales	Brassicaceae	*Brassica juncea*	X	
Capparales	Brassicaceae	*Cardamine hirsuta*	X	
Capparales	Brassicaceae	*Descurainia pinnata*	X	
Capparales	Brassicaceae	*Lepidium virginicum*	X	
Capparales	Brassicaceae	*Rorippa nasturtium-aquaticum*	X	
Bromeliales	Bromeliaceae	*Tillandsia usneoides*	X	
Scrophulariales	Buddlejaceae	*Polypremum procumbens*	X	X
Caryophyllales	Cactaceae	*Opuntia ficus-indica*	X	
Laurales	Calycanthaceae	*Calycanthus floridus var. floridus*	X	
Campanulales	Campanulaceae	*Lobelia elongata*	X	
Campanulales	Campanulaceae	*Lobelia glandulosa*	X	
Campanulales	Campanulaceae	*Lobelia nuttallii*	X	
Campanulales	Campanulaceae	*Specularia perfoliata*	X	
Dipsacales	Caprifoliaceae	*Lonicera japonica*	X	
Dipsacales	Caprifoliaceae	*Lonicera sempervirens*	X	
Dipsacales	Caprifoliaceae	*Sambucus canadensis*	X	
Dipsacales	Caprifoliaceae	*Viburnum dentatum*		X
Dipsacales	Caprifoliaceae	*Viburnum dentatum var. lucidum*	X	
Dipsacales	Caprifoliaceae	*Viburnum nudum*	X	
Dipsacales	Caprifoliaceae	*Viburnum rufidulum*	X	
Caryophyllales	Caryophyllaceae	*Cerastium glomeratum*	X	
Caryophyllales	Caryophyllaceae	*Cerastium holosteoides var. vulgare*	X	
Caryophyllales	Caryophyllaceae	*Paronychia riparia*	X	
Caryophyllales	Caryophyllaceae	*Silene antirrhina*	X	
Caryophyllales	Caryophyllaceae	*Stellaria media*	X	
Caryophyllales	Caryophyllaceae	*Stipulicida setacea*	X	
Celastrales	Celastraceae	*Celastrus orbiculatus*	X	
Celastrales	Celastraceae	*Euonymus americana*	X	
Caryophyllales	Chenopodiaceae	*Chenopodium ambrosioides*	X	
Caryophyllales	Chenopodiaceae	*Chenopodium botrys*	X	
Violales	Cistaceae	*Helianthemum canadense*	X	
Violales	Cistaceae	*Helianthemum carolinianum*	X	
Violales	Cistaceae	*Lechea leggettii*	X	
Violales	Cistaceae	*Lechea mucronata*	X	
Violales	Cistaceae	*Lechea pulchella*	X	
Ericales	Clethraceae	*Clethra alnifolia*	X	X

Table A-1. Continued.

Order	Family	Species	NPSpecies	This Study
Ericales	Clethraceae	*Clethra alnifolia*	X	X
Theales	Clusiaceae	*Hypericum cistifolium*	X	X
Theales	Clusiaceae	*Hypericum crux-andreae*	X	
Theales	Clusiaceae	*Hypericum densiflorum*	X	
Theales	Clusiaceae	*Hypericum galioides*	X	
Theales	Clusiaceae	*Hypericum gentianoides*	X	
Theales	Clusiaceae	*Hypericum hypericoides*	X	X
Theales	Clusiaceae	*Hypericum mutilum*	X	
Theales	Clusiaceae	*Hypericum setosum*	X	
Theales	Clusiaceae	*Triadenum walteri*	X	X
Commelinales	Commelinaceae	*Commelina communis*	X	
Commelinales	Commelinaceae	*Commelina diffusa*	X	
Commelinales	Commelinaceae	*Commelina erecta*	X	
Commelinales	Commelinaceae	*Murdannia keisak*	X	
Commelinales	Commelinaceae	*Tradescantia ohiensis*	X	
Commelinales	Commelinaceae	*Tradescantia rosea var. graminea*	X	
Solanales	Convolvulaceae	*Dichondra carolinensis*	X	
Solanales	Convolvulaceae	*Ipomoea coccinea*	X	
Solanales	Convolvulaceae	*Ipomoea hederacea*	X	
Solanales	Convolvulaceae	*Ipomoea hederacea var. integriuscula*	X	
Solanales	Convolvulaceae	*Ipomoea lacunosa*	X	
Solanales	Convolvulaceae	*Ipomoea pandurata*	X	
Solanales	Convolvulaceae	*Ipomoea purpurea*	X	
Solanales	Convolvulaceae	*Ipomoea trichocarpa*	X	
Solanales	Convolvulaceae	*Jacquemontia tamnifolia*	X	
Solanales	Convolvulaceae	*Stylisma humistrata*	X	
Cornales	Cornaceae	*Cornus florida*	X	X
Cornales	Cornaceae	*Cornus foemina*	X	
Violales	Cucurbitaceae	*Citrullus vulgaris*	X	
Pinales	Cupressaceae	*Chamaecyparis thyoides*	X	
Pinales	Cupressaceae	*Juniperus virginiana*	X	
Solanales	Cuscutaceae	*Cuscuta compacta*	X	
Cyperales	Cyperaceae	*Carex albolutescens*	X	
Cyperales	Cyperaceae	*Carex bullata*	X	
Cyperales	Cyperaceae	*Carex caroliniana*	X	
Cyperales	Cyperaceae	*Carex complanata*	X	
Cyperales	Cyperaceae	*Carex debilis*	X	
Cyperales	Cyperaceae	*Carex debilis var. pubera*	X	
Cyperales	Cyperaceae	*Carex folliculata*	X	
Cyperales	Cyperaceae	*Carex folliculata var. australis*	X	
Cyperales	Cyperaceae	*Carex glaucescens*	X	
Cyperales	Cyperaceae	*Carex howei*	X	
Cyperales	Cyperaceae	*Carex intumescens*	X	
Cyperales	Cyperaceae	*Carex lonchocarpa*	X	
Cyperales	Cyperaceae	*Carex lurida*	X	
Cyperales	Cyperaceae	*Carex nigromarginata*	X	
Cyperales	Cyperaceae	*Carex seorsa*	X	
Cyperales	Cyperaceae	*Carex venusta*	X	
Cyperales	Cyperaceae	*Cladium jamaicense*	X	
Cyperales	Cyperaceae	*Cyperus compressus*	X	
Cyperales	Cyperaceae	*Cyperus croceus*	X	

Table A-1. Continued.

Order	Family	Species	NPSpecies	This Study
Cyperales	Cyperaceae	*Cyperus haspan*	X	
Cyperales	Cyperaceae	*Cyperus iria*	X	
Cyperales	Cyperaceae	*Cyperus plukenetii*	X	
Cyperales	Cyperaceae	*Cyperus polystachyos var. texensis*	X	
Cyperales	Cyperaceae	*Cyperus retrorsus var. retrorsus*	X	
Cyperales	Cyperaceae	*Cyperus rotundus*	X	
Cyperales	Cyperaceae	*Cyperus strigosus*	X	
Cyperales	Cyperaceae	*Dulichium arundinaceum*	X	
Cyperales	Cyperaceae	*Eleocharis acicularis*	X	
Cyperales	Cyperaceae	*Eleocharis microcarpa*	X	
Cyperales	Cyperaceae	*Eleocharis obtusa*	X	
Cyperales	Cyperaceae	*Eleocharis tuberculosa*	X	
Cyperales	Cyperaceae	*Fuirena pumila*	X	
Cyperales	Cyperaceae	*Rhynchospora berteroi*	X	
Cyperales	Cyperaceae	*Rhynchospora caduca*	X	
Cyperales	Cyperaceae	*Rhynchospora chalarocephala*	X	
Cyperales	Cyperaceae	*Rhynchospora chapmanii*	X	
Cyperales	Cyperaceae	*Rhynchospora ciliaris*	X	
Cyperales	Cyperaceae	*Rhynchospora corniculata*	X	
Cyperales	Cyperaceae	*Rhynchospora debilis*	X	
Cyperales	Cyperaceae	*Rhynchospora fascicularis*	X	
Cyperales	Cyperaceae	*Rhynchospora globularis var. globularis*	X	
Cyperales	Cyperaceae	*Rhynchospora gracilenta*	X	
Cyperales	Cyperaceae	*Rhynchospora inexpansa*	X	
Cyperales	Cyperaceae	*Rhynchospora nitens*	X	
Cyperales	Cyperaceae	*Rhynchospora rariflora*	X	
Cyperales	Cyperaceae	*Rhynchospora stenophylla*	X	
Cyperales	Cyperaceae	*Scirpus cyperinus*	X	
Cyperales	Cyperaceae	*Scleria muehlenbergii*	X	
Cyperales	Cyperaceae	*Scleria pauciflora var. caroliniana*	X	
Cyperales	Cyperaceae	*Scleria triglomerata*	X	X
Ericales	Cyrillaceae	*Cyrilla racemiflora*	X	X
Polypodiales	Dennstaedtiaceae	*Pteridium aquilinum*	X	X
Liliales	Dioscoreaceae	*Dioscorea villosa*	X	
Nepenthales	Droseraceae	*Dionaea muscipula*	X	
Nepenthales	Droseraceae	*Drosera brevifolia*	X	
Nepenthales	Droseraceae	*Drosera capillaris*	X	
Nepenthales	Droseraceae	*Drosera intermedia*	X	
Polypodiales	Dryopteridaceae	*Athyrium asplenioides*	X	
Polypodiales	Dryopteridaceae	*Onoclea sensibilis*	X	X
Ebenales	Ebenaceae	*Diospyros virginiana*	X	X
Rhamnales	Elaeagnaceae	*Elaeagnus pungens*	X	
Ericales	Ericaceae	*Epigaea repens*	X	
Ericales	Ericaceae	*Gaylussacia dumosa*	X	X
Ericales	Ericaceae	*Gaylussacia frondosa*		X
Ericales	Ericaceae	*Gaylussacia frondosa var. frondosa*	X	
Ericales	Ericaceae	*Kalmia angustifolia var. carolina*	X	
Ericales	Ericaceae	*Leucothoe racemosa*	X	X
Ericales	Ericaceae	*Lyonia ligustrina*	X	X
Ericales	Ericaceae	*Lyonia lucida*	X	X
Ericales	Ericaceae	*Lyonia mariana*	X	

Table A-1. Continued.

Order	Family	Species	NPSpecies	This Study
Ericales	Ericaceae	*Rhododendron atlanticum*	X	
Ericales	Ericaceae	*Rhododendron canescens*	X	
Ericales	Ericaceae	*Rhododendron periclymenoides*	X	
Ericales	Ericaceae	*Vaccinium arboreum*	X	X
Ericales	Ericaceae	*Vaccinium corymbosum*	X	X
Ericales	Ericaceae	*Vaccinium crassifolium*	X	X
Ericales	Ericaceae	*Vaccinium elliottii*	X	X
Ericales	Ericaceae	*Vaccinium fuscatum*	X	
Ericales	Ericaceae	*Vaccinium pallidum*	X	
Ericales	Ericaceae	*Vaccinium stamineum*	X	
Ericales	Ericaceae	*Vaccinium tenellum*	X	
Eriocaulales	Eriocaulaceae	*Eriocaulon decangulare*	X	
Eriocaulales	Eriocaulaceae	*Lachnocaulon anceps*	X	
Euphorbiales	Euphorbiaceae	*Acalypha gracilens*	X	X
Euphorbiales	Euphorbiaceae	*Acalypha rhomboidea*	X	
Euphorbiales	Euphorbiaceae	*Chamaesyce maculata*	X	X
Euphorbiales	Euphorbiaceae	*Cnidoscolus stimulosus*	X	
Euphorbiales	Euphorbiaceae	*Croton glandulosus*	X	
Euphorbiales	Euphorbiaceae	*Euphorbia corollata*	X	
Euphorbiales	Euphorbiaceae	*Euphorbia curtisii*	X	
Euphorbiales	Euphorbiaceae	*Euphorbia ipecacuanhae*	X	
Euphorbiales	Euphorbiaceae	*Ricinus communis*	X	
Euphorbiales	Euphorbiaceae	*Stillingia sylvatica*	X	
Euphorbiales	Euphorbiaceae	*Tragia urens*	X	
Fabales	Fabaceae	*Albizia julibrissin*	X	
Fabales	Fabaceae	*Amorpha fruticosa*	X	
Fabales	Fabaceae	*Amorpha herbacea*	X	
Fabales	Fabaceae	*Baptisia tinctoria*	X	
Fabales	Fabaceae	*Cassia fasciculata*	X	
Fabales	Fabaceae	*Cassia nictitans*	X	
Fabales	Fabaceae	*Centrosema virginianum*	X	
Fabales	Fabaceae	*Cercis canadensis*	X	
Fabales	Fabaceae	*Clitoria mariana*	X	
Fabales	Fabaceae	*Crotalaria rotundifolia*	X	
Fabales	Fabaceae	*Crotalaria spectabilis*	X	
Fabales	Fabaceae	*Desmodium marilandicum*	X	
Fabales	Fabaceae	*Desmodium paniculatum*	X	
Fabales	Fabaceae	*Desmodium perplexum*	X	
Fabales	Fabaceae	*Galactia elliottii*		X
Fabales	Fabaceae	*Galactia regularis*	X	
Fabales	Fabaceae	*Galactia volubilis*	X	
Fabales	Fabaceae	*Indigofera caroliniana*	X	
Fabales	Fabaceae	*Kummerowia striata*	X	
Fabales	Fabaceae	*Lathyrus latifolius*	X	
Fabales	Fabaceae	*Lespedeza angustifolia*	X	
Fabales	Fabaceae	*Lespedeza capitata*	X	
Fabales	Fabaceae	*Lespedeza cuneata*	X	
Fabales	Fabaceae	*Lespedeza sp.*	X	X
Fabales	Fabaceae	*Lespedeza stuevei*	X	
Fabales	Fabaceae	*Lespedeza virginica*	X	
Fabales	Fabaceae	*Lupinus perennis*	X	

Table A-1. Continued.

Order	Family	Species	NPSpecies	This Study
Fabales	Fabaceae	*Lupinus villosus*	X	
Fabales	Fabaceae	*Medicago lupulina*	X	
Fabales	Fabaceae	*Medicago sp.*	X	X
Fabales	Fabaceae	*Melilotus alba*	X	
Fabales	Fabaceae	*Psoralea psoralioides*	X	
Fabales	Fabaceae	*Pueraria lobata*	X	
Fabales	Fabaceae	*Rhynchosia difformis*	X	
Fabales	Fabaceae	*Rhynchosia reniformis*	X	
Fabales	Fabaceae	*Robinia elliottii*	X	
Fabales	Fabaceae	*Robinia nana*	X	
Fabales	Fabaceae	*Senna obtusifolia*	X	
Fabales	Fabaceae	*Strophostyles umbellata*	X	
Fabales	Fabaceae	*Stylosanthes biflora*	X	
Fabales	Fabaceae	*Tephrosia hispidula*	X	
Fabales	Fabaceae	*Tephrosia spicata*	X	
Fabales	Fabaceae	*Trifolium arvense*	X	
Fabales	Fabaceae	*Trifolium campestre*	X	
Fabales	Fabaceae	*Trifolium dubium*	X	
Fabales	Fabaceae	*Trifolium hybridum*	X	
Fabales	Fabaceae	*Trifolium repens*	X	
Fabales	Fabaceae	*Vicia angustifolia*	X	
Fabales	Fabaceae	*Vicia sativa*	X	
Fabales	Fabaceae	*Wisteria floribunda*	X	
Fabales	Fabaceae	*Wisteria frutescens*	X	
Fabales	Fabaceae	*Wisteria sinensis*	X	X
Fabales	Fabaceae	*Zornia bracteata*	X	
Fagales	Fagaceae	*Castanea pumila var. pumila*	X	
Fagales	Fagaceae	*Fagus grandifolia*	X	
Fagales	Fagaceae	*Quercus alba*	X	
Fagales	Fagaceae	*Quercus coccinea*	X	
Fagales	Fagaceae	*Quercus falcata*	X	X
Fagales	Fagaceae	*Quercus falcata var. falcata*	X	
Fagales	Fagaceae	*Quercus falcata var. pagodifolia*	X	
Fagales	Fagaceae	*Quercus incana*	X	
Fagales	Fagaceae	*Quercus laevis*	X	
Fagales	Fagaceae	*Quercus laurifolia*	X	X
Fagales	Fagaceae	*Quercus lyrata*	X	X
Fagales	Fagaceae	*Quercus margarettiae*	X	
Fagales	Fagaceae	*Quercus marilandica*	X	
Fagales	Fagaceae	*Quercus michauxii*	X	
Fagales	Fagaceae	*Quercus myrtifolia*	X	
Fagales	Fagaceae	*Quercus nigra*	X	X
Fagales	Fagaceae	*Quercus phellos*	X	
Fagales	Fagaceae	*Quercus rubra*	X	
Fagales	Fagaceae	*Quercus stellata*	X	X
Fagales	Fagaceae	*Quercus velutina*	X	
Gentianales	Gentianaceae	*Bartonia virginica*	X	
Gentianales	Gentianaceae	*Gentiana autumnalis*	X	
Gentianales	Gentianaceae	*Gentiana catesbaei*	X	
Gentianales	Gentianaceae	*Sabatia brachiata*	X	
Gentianales	Gentianaceae	*Sabatia campanulata*	X	

Table A-1. Continued.

Order	Family	Species	NPSpecies	This Study
Gentianales	Gentianaceae	*Sabatia difformis*	X	
Geraniales	Geraniaceae	*Geranium carolinianum*	X	
Rosales	Grossulariaceae	*Itea virginica*	X	X
Liliales	Haemodoraceae	*Lachnanthes caroliana*	X	
Haloragales	Haloragaceae	*Proserpinaca palustris*	X	
Hamamelidales	Hamamelidaceae	*Hamamelis virginiana*	X	
Hamamelidales	Hamamelidaceae	*Liquidambar styraciflua*	X	X
Rosales	Hydrangeaceae	*Decumaria barbara*	X	
Liliales	Iridaceae	*Gladiolus X gandavensis*	X	
Liliales	Iridaceae	*Hypoxis hirsuta var. leptocarpa*	X	X
Liliales	Iridaceae	*Hypoxis wrightii*	X	
Liliales	Iridaceae	*Iris verna*	X	
Liliales	Iridaceae	*Iris verna var. verna*	X	
Liliales	Iridaceae	*Iris virginica*	X	
Liliales	Iridaceae	*Sisyrinchium fuscatum*	X	
Liliales	Iridaceae	*Sisyrinchium mucronatum var. atlanticum*	X	
Liliales	Iridaceae	*Sisyrinchium rosulatum*	X	
Juglandales	Juglandaceae	*Carya alba*	X	X
Juglandales	Juglandaceae	*Carya glabra*	X	
Juglandales	Juglandaceae	*Carya pallida*	X	
Juncales	Juncaceae	*Juncus acuminatus*	X	
Juncales	Juncaceae	*Juncus biflorus*	X	
Juncales	Juncaceae	*Juncus canadensis*	X	
Juncales	Juncaceae	*Juncus coriaceus*	X	
Juncales	Juncaceae	*Juncus dichotomus*	X	
Juncales	Juncaceae	*Juncus diffusissimus*	X	
Juncales	Juncaceae	*Juncus effusus*	X	
Juncales	Juncaceae	*Juncus elliottii*	X	
Juncales	Juncaceae	*Juncus polycephalus*	X	
Juncales	Juncaceae	*Juncus scirpoides var. 2*	X	
Juncales	Juncaceae	*Juncus tenuis*	X	
Juncales	Juncaceae	*Juncus trigonocarpus*	X	
Lamiales	Lamiaceae	*Dracocephalum virginianum*	X	
Lamiales	Lamiaceae	*Glechoma hederacea*	X	
Lamiales	Lamiaceae	*Hyptis alata*	X	
Lamiales	Lamiaceae	*Lamium amplexicaule*	X	
Lamiales	Lamiaceae	*Lycopus rubellus*	X	
Lamiales	Lamiaceae	*Lycopus rubellus var. rubellus*	X	
Lamiales	Lamiaceae	*Lycopus virginicus*	X	
Lamiales	Lamiaceae	*Macbridea caroliniana*	X	
Lamiales	Lamiaceae	*Physostegia purpurea*	X	
Lamiales	Lamiaceae	*Prunella vulgaris*	X	
Lamiales	Lamiaceae	*Pycnanthemum muticum*	X	
Lamiales	Lamiaceae	*Pycnanthemum tenuifolium*	X	
Lamiales	Lamiaceae	*Salvia lyrata*	X	
Lamiales	Lamiaceae	*Scutellaria integrifolia*	X	
Lamiales	Lamiaceae	*Scutellaria integrifolia var. integrifolia*	X	
Lamiales	Lamiaceae	*Trichostema dichotomum*	X	
Laurales	Lauraceae	*Persea borbonia*		X
Laurales	Lauraceae	*Persea palustris*	X	X
Laurales	Lauraceae	*Sassafras albidum*	X	X

Table A-1. Continued.

Order	Family	Species	NPSpecies	This Study
Scrophulariales	Lentibulariaceae	*Pinguicula caerulea*	X	
Scrophulariales	Lentibulariaceae	*Pinguicula lutea*	X	
Scrophulariales	Lentibulariaceae	*Utricularia subulata*	X	
Liliales	Liliaceae	*Aletris aurea*	X	
Liliales	Liliaceae	*Aletris farinosa*	X	
Liliales	Liliaceae	*Allium vineale*	X	
Liliales	Liliaceae	*Hemerocallis fulva*	X	
Liliales	Liliaceae	*Hymenocallis floridana*	X	X
Liliales	Liliaceae	*Lilium catesbaei*	X	
Liliales	Liliaceae	*Lilium catesbaei var. longii*	X	
Liliales	Liliaceae	*Melanthium virginicum*	X	
Liliales	Liliaceae	*Narcissus tazetta X poeticus*	X	
Liliales	Liliaceae	*Ornithogalum umbellatum*	X	
Liliales	Liliaceae	*Tofieldia glabra*	X	
Liliales	Liliaceae	*Tofieldia racemosa*	X	
Liliales	Liliaceae	*Zigadenus glaberrimus*	X	
Linales	Linaceae	*Linum medium var. medium*	X	
Linales	Linaceae	*Linum striatum*	X	
Linales	Linaceae	*Linum virginianum*	X	
Gentianales	Loganiaceae	*Gelsemium rankinii*	X	
Gentianales	Loganiaceae	*Gelsemium sempervirens*	X	X
Gentianales	Loganiaceae	*Mitreola sessilifolia*	X	
Lycopodiales	Lycopodiaceae	*Lycopodiella alopecuroides*	X	
Lycopodiales	Lycopodiaceae	*Lycopodium appressum*	X	
Lycopodiales	Lycopodiaceae	*Lycopodium carolinianum*	X	
Myrtales	Lythraceae	*Cuphea carthagenensis*	X	
Myrtales	Lythraceae	*Lagerstroemia indica*	X	
Magnoliales	Magnoliaceae	*Liriodendron tulipifera*	X	X
Magnoliales	Magnoliaceae	*Magnolia grandiflora*	X	X
Magnoliales	Magnoliaceae	*Magnolia virginiana*	X	X
Malvales	Malvaceae	*Sida rhombifolia*	X	
Myrtales	Melastomataceae	*Rhexia alifanus*	X	
Myrtales	Melastomataceae	*Rhexia lutea*	X	
Myrtales	Melastomataceae	*Rhexia mariana*	X	
Myrtales	Melastomataceae	*Rhexia petiolata*	X	
Myrtales	Melastomataceae	*Rhexia virginica*		X
Sapindales	Meliaceae	*Melia azedarach*	X	
Caryophyllales	Molluginaceae	*Mollugo verticillata*	X	
Urticales	Moraceae	*Ficus carica*	X	
Myricales	Myricaceae	*Morella caroliniensis*	X	
Myricales	Myricaceae	*Morella cerifera*	X	X
Nymphaeales	Nymphaeaceae	*Nuphar lutea ssp. sagittifolia*	X	
Cornales	Nyssaceae	*Nyssa aquatica*	X	
Cornales	Nyssaceae	*Nyssa biflora*	X	X
Cornales	Nyssaceae	*Nyssa sylvatica*	X	X
Cornales	Nyssaceae	*Nyssa sylvatica var. biflora*	X	
Cornales	Nyssaceae	*Nyssa sylvatica var. sylvatica*	X	
Scrophulariales	Oleaceae	*Chionanthus virginicus*	X	
Scrophulariales	Oleaceae	*Fraxinus caroliniana*	X	X
Scrophulariales	Oleaceae	*Fraxinus pennsylvanica*		X
Scrophulariales	Oleaceae	*Ligustrum japonicum*	X	

Table A-1. Continued.

Order	Family	Species	NPSpecies	This Study
Scrophulariales	Oleaceae	*Ligustrum lucidum*	X	
Scrophulariales	Oleaceae	*Ligustrum sinense*	X	X
Scrophulariales	Oleaceae	*Osmanthus americanus*	X	
Myrtales	Onagraceae	*Ludwigia alternifolia*	X	
Myrtales	Onagraceae	*Ludwigia decurrens*	X	
Myrtales	Onagraceae	*Ludwigia glandulosa*	X	
Myrtales	Onagraceae	*Ludwigia maritima*	X	
Myrtales	Onagraceae	*Ludwigia palustris*	X	
Myrtales	Onagraceae	*Ludwigia repens*	X	
Myrtales	Onagraceae	*Ludwigia virgata*	X	
Myrtales	Onagraceae	*Oenothera biennis*	X	
Myrtales	Onagraceae	*Oenothera fruticosa*	X	
Myrtales	Onagraceae	*Oenothera laciniata*	X	
Myrtales	Onagraceae	*Oenothera laciniata laciniata*	X	
Myrtales	Onagraceae	*Oenothera tetragona*	X	
Orchidales	Orchidaceae	*Calopogon pulchellus*	X	
Orchidales	Orchidaceae	*Cleistes divaricata*	X	
Orchidales	Orchidaceae	*Habenaria blephariglottis*	X	
Orchidales	Orchidaceae	*Isotria verticillata*	X	
Orchidales	Orchidaceae	*Malaxis unifolia*	X	
Orchidales	Orchidaceae	*Platanthera ciliaris*	X	
Orchidales	Orchidaceae	*Platanthera cristata*	X	
Orchidales	Orchidaceae	*Pogonia ophioglossoides*	X	
Orchidales	Orchidaceae	*Spiranthes cernua*	X	
Orchidales	Orchidaceae	*Spiranthes gracilis*	X	
Orchidales	Orchidaceae	*Spiranthes praecox*	X	
Orchidales	Orchidaceae	*Tipularia discolor*	X	
Polypodiales	Osmundaceae	*Osmunda cinnamomea*	X	X
Polypodiales	Osmundaceae	*Osmunda regalis var. spectabilis*	X	X
Geraniales	Oxalidaceae	*Oxalis corniculata*		X
Geraniales	Oxalidaceae	*Oxalis rubra*	X	
Geraniales	Oxalidaceae	*Oxalis stricta*	X	
Violales	Passifloraceae	*Passiflora incarnata*	X	
Caryophyllales	Phytolaccaceae	*Phytolacca americana*	X	
Pinales	Pinaceae	*Pinus palustris*	X	X
Pinales	Pinaceae	*Pinus serotina*	X	
Pinales	Pinaceae	*Pinus taeda*	X	X
Plantaginales	Plantaginaceae	*Plantago aristata*	X	
Plantaginales	Plantaginaceae	*Plantago lanceolata*	X	
Plantaginales	Plantaginaceae	*Plantago rugelii*	X	
Plantaginales	Plantaginaceae	*Plantago virginica*	X	
Hamamelidales	Platanaceae	*Platanus occidentalis*	X	
Cyperales	Poaceae	*Agrostis hyemalis*	X	
Cyperales	Poaceae	*Andropogon scoparius*	X	
Cyperales	Poaceae	*Andropogon ternarius*	X	
Cyperales	Poaceae	*Andropogon virginicus*	X	
Cyperales	Poaceae	*Anthoxanthum odoratum*	X	
Cyperales	Poaceae	*Aristida stricta*	X	X
Cyperales	Poaceae	*Aristida virgata*	X	
Cyperales	Poaceae	*Arundinaria gigantea*	X	X
Cyperales	Poaceae	*Arundinaria tecta*	X	

Table A-1. Continued.

Order	Family	Species	NPSpecies	This Study
Cyperales	Poaceae	*Axonopus fissifolius*	X	
Cyperales	Poaceae	*Axonopus furcatus*	X	
Cyperales	Poaceae	*Calamagrostis coarctata*	X	
Cyperales	Poaceae	*Cenchrus tribuloides*	X	
Cyperales	Poaceae	*Chasmanthium laxum*	X	X
Cyperales	Poaceae	*Ctenium aromaticum*	X	
Cyperales	Poaceae	*Cynodon dactylon*	X	
Cyperales	Poaceae	*Dactylis glomerata*	X	
Cyperales	Poaceae	*Danthonia sericea*	X	
Cyperales	Poaceae	*Danthonia sericea var. sericea*	X	
Cyperales	Poaceae	*Dichanthelium acuminatum var. lindheimeri*	X	
Cyperales	Poaceae	*Dichanthelium commutatum*	X	
Cyperales	Poaceae	*Dichanthelium dichotomum var. dichotomum*	X	
Cyperales	Poaceae	*Dichanthelium ensifolium*	X	
Cyperales	Poaceae	*Dichanthelium erectifolium*	X	
Cyperales	Poaceae	*Dichanthelium laxiflorum*	X	
Cyperales	Poaceae	*Dichanthelium sphaerocarpon*	X	
Cyperales	Poaceae	*Dichanthelium strigosum var. strigosum*	X	
Cyperales	Poaceae	*Dichanthelium villosissimum*	X	
Cyperales	Poaceae	*Digitaria sanguinalis*	X	
Cyperales	Poaceae	*Echinochloa crus-galli*	X	
Cyperales	Poaceae	*Elymus virginicus*	X	
Cyperales	Poaceae	*Eragrostis capillaris*	X	
Cyperales	Poaceae	*Eragrostis refracta*	X	
Cyperales	Poaceae	*Eragrostis spectabilis*	X	
Cyperales	Poaceae	*Eremochloa ophiuroides*	X	X
Cyperales	Poaceae	*Erianthus brevibarbis*	X	
Cyperales	Poaceae	*Erianthus contortus*	X	
Cyperales	Poaceae	*Festuca elatior var. arundinacea*	X	
Cyperales	Poaceae	*Festuca octoflora*	X	
Cyperales	Poaceae	*Hordeum pusillum*	X	
Cyperales	Poaceae	*Leersia oryzoides*	X	
Cyperales	Poaceae	*Lolium multiflorum*	X	
Cyperales	Poaceae	*Lolium pratense*	X	
Cyperales	Poaceae	*Panicum agrostoides*	X	
Cyperales	Poaceae	*Panicum anceps*	X	
Cyperales	Poaceae	*Panicum ensifolium*	X	
Cyperales	Poaceae	*Panicum rigidulum var. pubescens*	X	
Cyperales	Poaceae	*Panicum sphaerocarpon*	X	
Cyperales	Poaceae	*Panicum tenue*	X	
Cyperales	Poaceae	*Panicum verrucosum*	X	
Cyperales	Poaceae	*Panicum villosissimum*	X	
Cyperales	Poaceae	*Paspalum dilatatum*	X	
Cyperales	Poaceae	*Paspalum distichum*	X	
Cyperales	Poaceae	*Paspalum floridanum*	X	
Cyperales	Poaceae	*Paspalum laeve*	X	
Cyperales	Poaceae	*Paspalum notatum*		X
Cyperales	Poaceae	*Paspalum notatum var. saurae*	X	
Cyperales	Poaceae	*Paspalum setaceum*	X	
Cyperales	Poaceae	*Paspalum urvillei*	X	
Cyperales	Poaceae	*Poa annua*	X	

Table A-1. Continued.

Order	Family	Species	NPSpecies	This Study
Cyperales	Poaceae	*Poa pratensis*	X	
Cyperales	Poaceae	*Saccharum baldwinii*	X	
Cyperales	Poaceae	*Saccharum brevibarbe var. brevibarbe*	X	
Cyperales	Poaceae	*Schizachyrium tenerum*	X	
Cyperales	Poaceae	*Setaria parviflora*	X	
Cyperales	Poaceae	*Sphenopholis obtusata*	X	
Cyperales	Poaceae	*Sporobolus poiretii*	X	
Cyperales	Poaceae	*Tridens flavus var. flavus*	X	
Cyperales	Poaceae	*Vulpia myuros*	X	
Cyperales	Poaceae	*Vulpia sciurea*	X	
Solanales	Polemoniaceae	*Phlox nivalis*	X	
Polygalales	Polygalaceae	*Polygala cruciata*	X	
Polygalales	Polygalaceae	*Polygala cymosa*	X	
Polygalales	Polygalaceae	*Polygala lutea*	X	
Polygonales	Polygonaceae	*Polygonum hydropiper*	X	
Polygonales	Polygonaceae	*Polygonum hydropiperoides*	X	
Polygonales	Polygonaceae	*Polygonum hydropiperoides hydropiperoides*	X	
Polygonales	Polygonaceae	*Polygonum hydropiperoides var. opelousanum*	X	
Polygonales	Polygonaceae	*Polygonum pensylvanicum*	X	
Polygonales	Polygonaceae	*Polygonum sagittatum*	X	
Polygonales	Polygonaceae	*Rumex acetosella*	X	
Polygonales	Polygonaceae	*Rumex crispus*	X	
Polygonales	Polygonaceae	*Rumex hastatulus*	X	
Polypodiales	Polypodiaceae	*Polypodium polypodioides*	X	
Liliales	Pontederiaceae	*Pontederia cordata*	X	
Caryophyllales	Portulacaceae	*Portulaca pilosa*	X	
Primulales	Primulaceae	*Lysimachia X producta*	X	
Ericales	Pyrolaceae	*Chimaphila maculata*	X	
Ranunculales	Ranunculaceae	*Clematis crispa*	X	
Ranunculales	Ranunculaceae	*Clematis ochroleuca*	X	
Ranunculales	Ranunculaceae	*Ranunculus bulbosus*	X	
Ranunculales	Ranunculaceae	*Thalictrum macrostylum*	X	
Ranunculales	Ranunculaceae	*Xanthorhiza simplicissima*	X	
Rosales	Rosaceae	*Amelanchier obovalis*	X	
Rosales	Rosaceae	*Amelanchier stolonifera*	X	
Rosales	Rosaceae	*Crataegus aestivalis*	X	
Rosales	Rosaceae	*Crataegus flava*	X	
Rosales	Rosaceae	*Duchesnea indica*	X	
Rosales	Rosaceae	*Fragaria X ananassa*	X	
Rosales	Rosaceae	*Photinia pyrifolia*	X	X
Rosales	Rosaceae	*Potentilla canadensis*	X	X
Rosales	Rosaceae	*Potentilla simplex*	X	
Rosales	Rosaceae	*Prunus angustifolia*	X	
Rosales	Rosaceae	*Prunus serotina var. serotina*	X	X
Rosales	Rosaceae	*Pyrus communis*	X	
Rosales	Rosaceae	*Rosa multiflora*	X	
Rosales	Rosaceae	*Rosa palustris*	X	
Rosales	Rosaceae	*Rosa X noisettiana*	X	
Rosales	Rosaceae	*Rubus argutus*		X
Rosales	Rosaceae	*Rubus cuneifolius*	X	
Rosales	Rosaceae	*Rubus hispidus*	X	

Table A-1. Continued.

Order	Family	Species	NPSpecies	This Study
Rosales	Rosaceae	*Rubus pubescens* var. *pubescens*	X	
Rosales	Rosaceae	*Rubus trivialis*	X	
Rosales	Rosaceae	*Sorbus arbutifolia* var. *arbutifolia*	X	
Rosales	Rosaceae	*Spiraea thunbergii*	X	
Rubiales	Rubiaceae	*Cephalanthus occidentalis*	X	
Rubiales	Rubiaceae	*Diodia teres*	X	X
Rubiales	Rubiaceae	*Diodia virginiana*	X	
Rubiales	Rubiaceae	*Galium aparine*		X
Rubiales	Rubiaceae	*Galium obtusum*	X	
Rubiales	Rubiaceae	*Galium obtusum* ssp. *filifolium*	X	
Rubiales	Rubiaceae	*Galium pilosum*	X	
Rubiales	Rubiaceae	*Galium tinctorium*	X	
Rubiales	Rubiaceae	*Houstonia pusilla*	X	
Rubiales	Rubiaceae	*Mitchella repens*	X	X
Rubiales	Rubiaceae	*Oldenlandia uniflora*	X	
Rubiales	Rubiaceae	*Richardia brasiliensis*	X	
Salicales	Salicaceae	*Populus heterophylla*	X	X
Salicales	Salicaceae	*Populus nigra*	X	
Salicales	Salicaceae	*Salix caroliniana*	X	X
Salicales	Salicaceae	*Salix nigra*	X	
Salicales	Salicaceae	*Salix X pendulina*	X	
Nepenthales	Sarraceniaceae	*Sarracenia flava*	X	
Nepenthales	Sarraceniaceae	*Sarracenia purpurea*	X	
Piperales	Saururaceae	*Saururus cernuus*	X	X
Rosales	Saxifragaceae	*Parnassia caroliniana*	X	
Scrophulariales	Scrophulariaceae	*Agalinis fasciculata*	X	
Scrophulariales	Scrophulariaceae	*Agalinis obtusifolia*	X	
Scrophulariales	Scrophulariaceae	*Agalinis purpurea*	X	
Scrophulariales	Scrophulariaceae	*Agalinis setacea*	X	
Scrophulariales	Scrophulariaceae	*Aureolaria pectinata*	X	
Scrophulariales	Scrophulariaceae	*Bacopa caroliniana*	X	
Scrophulariales	Scrophulariaceae	*Chelone glabra*	X	
Scrophulariales	Scrophulariaceae	*Gratiola aurea*	X	
Scrophulariales	Scrophulariaceae	*Gratiola pilosa*	X	
Scrophulariales	Scrophulariaceae	*Gratiola virginiana*	X	
Scrophulariales	Scrophulariaceae	*Mecardonia acuminata*	X	
Scrophulariales	Scrophulariaceae	*Nuttallanthus canadensis*	X	
Scrophulariales	Scrophulariaceae	*Pedicularis canadensis*	X	
Scrophulariales	Scrophulariaceae	*Penstemon australis*	X	
Scrophulariales	Scrophulariaceae	*Seymeria cassioides*	X	
Scrophulariales	Scrophulariaceae	*Verbascum thapsus*	X	
Scrophulariales	Scrophulariaceae	*Veronica arvensis*	X	
Scrophulariales	Scrophulariaceae	*Veronica peregrina*	X	
Selaginellales	Selaginellaceae	*Selaginella apoda*	X	
Liliales	Smilacaceae	*Smilax auriculata*	X	
Liliales	Smilacaceae	*Smilax bona-nox*	X	
Liliales	Smilacaceae	*Smilax glauca*	X	
Liliales	Smilacaceae	*Smilax herbacea*	X	
Liliales	Smilacaceae	*Smilax laurifolia*	X	
Liliales	Smilacaceae	*Smilax rotundifolia*	X	X
Liliales	Smilacaceae	*Smilax tamnoides*	X	

Table A-1. Continued.

Order	Family	Species	NPSpecies	This Study
Liliales	Smilacaceae	*Smilax walteri*	X	
Solanales	Solanaceae	*Physalis angulata*	X	
Solanales	Solanaceae	*Physalis virginiana*	X	
Solanales	Solanaceae	*Solanum americanum*	X	
Solanales	Solanaceae	*Solanum carolinense*	X	
Typhales	Sparganiaceae	*Sparganium americanum*	X	
Ebenales	Styracaceae	*Styrax americana*	X	
Ebenales	Symplocaceae	*Symplocos tinctoria*	X	X
Pinales	Taxodiaceae	*Taxodium ascendens*	X	X
Pinales	Taxodiaceae	*Taxodium distichum*	X	X
Theales	Theaceae	*Gordonia lasianthus*	X	
Typhales	Typhaceae	*Typha domingensis*	X	
Typhales	Typhaceae	*Typha latifolia*	X	
Urticales	Urticaceae	*Boehmeria cylindrica*	X	X
Dipsacales	Valerianaceae	*Valerianella radiata*	X	
Lamiales	Verbenaceae	*Callicarpa americana*	X	X
Lamiales	Verbenaceae	*Phyla nodiflora*	X	
Lamiales	Verbenaceae	*Stylodon carneus*	X	
Lamiales	Verbenaceae	*Verbena brasiliensis*	X	
Violales	Violaceae	*Viola affinis*	X	
Violales	Violaceae	*Viola brittoniana*	X	
Violales	Violaceae	*Viola brittoniana var. brittoniana*	X	
Violales	Violaceae	*Viola lanceolata*	X	
Violales	Violaceae	*Viola palmata*	X	
Violales	Violaceae	*Viola pedata*	X	
Violales	Violaceae	*Viola primulifolia*	X	
Violales	Violaceae	*Viola sororia*	X	
Violales	Violaceae	*Viola villosa*	X	
Santalales	Viscaceae	*Phoradendron leucarpum*	X	
Rhamnales	Vitaceae	*Parthenocissus quinquefolia*	X	X
Rhamnales	Vitaceae	*Vitis cinerea var. floridana*	X	
Rhamnales	Vitaceae	*Vitis rotundifolia*	X	X
Commelinales	Xyridaceae	*Xyris ambigua*	X	
Commelinales	Xyridaceae	*Xyris caroliniana*	X	
Commelinales	Xyridaceae	*Xyris difformis*	X	
Commelinales	Xyridaceae	*Xyris jupicai*	X	

Appendix B. Plant species detected in macroplots.

Table B-1. Vascular plant species detected in all macroplot inventories (i.e., across-macroplot species composition) at Moores Creek National Battlefield, 2010.

Order	Family	Species	Common Name
Sapindales	Aceraceae	*Acer rubrum*	red maple
Sapindales	Anacardiaceae	*Rhus copallina*	
Sapindales	Anacardiaceae	*Toxicodendron radicans*	eastern poison ivy, poison ivy, poisonivy
Apiales	Apiaceae	*Hydrocotyle umbellata*	
Celastrales	Aquifoliaceae	*Ilex coriacea*	large gallberry
Celastrales	Aquifoliaceae	*Ilex glabra*	inberry, inkberry
Celastrales	Aquifoliaceae	*Ilex opaca*	American holly
Celastrales	Aquifoliaceae	*Ilex vomitoria*	
Apiales	Araliaceae	*Aralia spinosa*	
Aristolochiales	Aristolochiaceae	*Hexastylis arifolia*	littlebrownjug
Polypodiales	Aspleniaceae	*Asplenium platyneuron*	ebony spleenwort
Asterales	Asteraceae	*Ambrosia artemisiifolia*	annual ragweed, common ragweed, low ragweed
Asterales	Asteraceae	*Conyza canadensis*	
Asterales	Asteraceae	*Erigeron vernus*	early whitetop fleabane
Asterales	Asteraceae	*Eupatorium capillifolium*	dogfennel
Asterales	Asteraceae	*Mikania scandens*	climbing hempvine, climbing hempweed
Fagales	Betulaceae	*Betula nigra*	river birch
Fagales	Betulaceae	*Carpinus caroliniana*	American hornbeam, american hornbean
Scrophulariales	Bignoniaceae	*Bignonia capreolata*	cross vine, crossvine
Scrophulariales	Bignoniaceae	*Campsis radicans*	common trumpetcreeper, cow-itch, trumpet creeper
Scrophulariales	Bignoniaceae	*Catalpa speciosa*	
Polypodiales	Blechnaceae	*Woodwardia areolata*	chainfern, netted chainfern
Polypodiales	Blechnaceae	*Woodwardia virginica*	virginia chainfern, Virginia chainfern
Scrophulariales	Buddlejaceae	*Polypremum procumbens*	juniper leaf
Dipsacales	Caprifoliaceae	*Viburnum dentatum*	
Ericales	Clethraceae	*Clethra alnifolia*	
Theales	Clusiaceae	*Hypericum cistifolium*	roundpod St. Johnswort
Theales	Clusiaceae	*Hypericum hypericoides*	St. Andrews cross, St. Andrew's cross
Theales	Clusiaceae	*Triadenum walteri*	greater marsh St. Johnswort
Cornales	Cornaceae	*Cornus florida*	flowering dogwood
Cyperales	Cyperaceae	*Scleria triglomerata*	whip nutrush
Ericales	Cyrillaceae	*Cyrilla racemiflora*	swamp cyrilla, swamp titi
Polypodiales	Dennstaedtiaceae	*Pteridium aquilinum*	bracken, bracken fern, brackenfern
Polypodiales	Dryopteridaceae	*Onoclea sensibilis*	sensitive fern
Ebenales	Ebenaceae	*Diospyros virginiana*	common persimmon, eastern persimmon, Persimmon
Ericales	Ericaceae	*Gaylussacia dumosa*	dwarf huckleberry
Ericales	Ericaceae	*Gaylussacia frondosa*	
Ericales	Ericaceae	*Leucothoe racemosa*	swamp doghobble
Ericales	Ericaceae	*Lyonia ligustrina*	he-huckleberry, maleberry
Ericales	Ericaceae	*Lyonia lucida*	fetterbush lyonia
Ericales	Ericaceae	*Vaccinium arboreum*	farkleberry, tree sparkleberry, tree-huckelberry
Ericales	Ericaceae	*Vaccinium corymbosum*	highbush blueberry

Table B-1. Continued.

Order	Family	Species	Common Name
Ericales	Ericaceae	*Vaccinium crassifolium*	creeping blueberry
Ericales	Ericaceae	*Vaccinium elliottii*	Elliott's blueberry
Fabales	Fabaceae	*Galactia elliottii*	
Fabales	Fabaceae	*Lespedeza sp.*	
Fabales	Fabaceae	*Wisteria sinensis*	Chinese wisteria
Fagales	Fagaceae	*Quercus falcata*	southern red oak
Fagales	Fagaceae	*Quercus laurifolia*	laurel oak
Fagales	Fagaceae	*Quercus lyrata*	overcup oak
Fagales	Fagaceae	*Quercus nigra*	water oak
Fagales	Fagaceae	*Quercus stellata*	post oak
Rosales	Grossulariaceae	*Itea virginica*	Virginia sweetspire
Hamamelidales	Hamamelidaceae	*Liquidambar styraciflua*	sweetgum
Juglandales	Juglandaceae	*Carya alba*	mockernut hickory
Laurales	Lauraceae	*Persea borbonia*	red bay
Laurales	Lauraceae	*Persea palustris*	swamp bay
Laurales	Lauraceae	*Sassafras albidum*	sassafras
Liliales	Liliaceae	*Hymenocallis floridana*	Florida spiderlily
Gentianales	Loganiaceae	*Gelsemium sempervirens*	Carolina jessamine, evening trumpetflower
Magnoliales	Magnoliaceae	*Liriodendron tulipifera*	tulip poplar, tuliptree, yellow poplar
Magnoliales	Magnoliaceae	*Magnolia grandiflora*	southern magnolia
Magnoliales	Magnoliaceae	*Magnolia virginiana*	sweetbay
Myrtales	Melastomataceae	*Rhexia virginica*	meadowbeauty
Myricales	Myricaceae	*Morella cerifera*	wax myrtle, waxmyrtle
Cornales	Nyssaceae	*Nyssa biflora*	swamp tupelo
Cornales	Nyssaceae	*Nyssa sylvatica*	black gum, black tupelo, blackgum
Scrophulariales	Oleaceae	*Fraxinus caroliniana*	Carolina ash
Scrophulariales	Oleaceae	*Fraxinus pennsylvanica*	green ash
Scrophulariales	Oleaceae	*Ligustrum sinense*	Chinese privet, common chinese privet
Polypodiales	Osmundaceae	*Osmunda cinnamomea*	cinnamon fern
Polypodiales	Osmundaceae	*Osmunda regalis var. spectabilis*	royal fern
Geraniales	Oxalidaceae	*Oxalis corniculata*	wood sorrel
Pinales	Pinaceae	*Pinus palustris*	longleaf pine
Pinales	Pinaceae	*Pinus taeda*	loblolly pine
Cyperales	Poaceae	*Aristida stricta*	pineland threeawn
Cyperales	Poaceae	*Arundinaria gigantea*	giant cane
Cyperales	Poaceae	*Chasmanthium laxum*	
Cyperales	Poaceae	*Eremochloa ophiuroides*	centipede grass
Cyperales	Poaceae	*Paspalum notatum*	bahiagrass
Rosales	Rosaceae	*Photinia pyrifolia*	red chokeberry
Rosales	Rosaceae	*Potentilla canadensis*	dwarf cinquefoil
Rosales	Rosaceae	*Prunus serotina var. serotina*	black cherry
Rosales	Rosaceae	*Rubus argutus*	
Rubiales	Rubiaceae	*Diodia teres*	poor joe, poorjoe, rough buttonweed
Rubiales	Rubiaceae	*Galium aparine*	bedstraw
Rubiales	Rubiaceae	*Mitchella repens*	partridgeberry

Table B-1. Continued.

Order	Family	Species	Common Name
Salicales	Salicaceae	*Populus heterophylla*	swamp cottonwood
Salicales	Salicaceae	*Salix caroliniana*	coastal plain willow
Piperales	Saururaceae	*Saururus cernuus*	lizards tail, lizard's tail
Liliales	Smilacaceae	*Smilax rotundifolia*	bullbriar, common catbriar, common greenbrier
Ebenales	Symplocaceae	*Symplocos tinctoria*	common sweetleaf, sweetleaf
Pinales	Taxodiaceae	*Taxodium distichum*	bald cypress, baldcypress
Urticales	Urticaceae	*Boehmeria cylindrica*	smallspike false nettle, small-spike false nettle, smallspike falsenettle
Lamiales	Verbenaceae	*Callicarpa americana*	American beautyberry
Rhamnales	Vitaceae	*Parthenocissus quinquefolia*	American ivy, fiveleaved ivy, Virginia creeper
Rhamnales	Vitaceae	*Vitis rotundifolia*	muscadine, muscadine grape

Table B-2. Vascular plant species detected in each macoplot inventory (i.e., within-macroplot species composition) at Moores Creek National Battlefield, 2010.

Sampling Location	Species
1	Acer rubrum
1	Arundinaria gigantea
1	Bignonia capreolata
1	Boehmeria cylindrica
1	Carya tomentosa
1	Chasmanthium laxum
1	Clethra alnifolia
1	Cornus florida
1	Elephantopus sp.
1	Eupatorium capillifolium
1	Galactia elliottii
1	Gaylussacia dumosa
1	Gelsemium sempervirens
1	Hexastylis arifolia
1	Hydrocotyle sp.
1	Hypericum cistifolium
1	Ilex coriacea
1	Ilex glabra
1	Ilex opaca
1	Juncus sp.
1	Leucothoe racemosa
1	Liquidambar styraciflua
1	Liriodendron tulipifera
1	Lyonia ligustrina
1	Lyonia lucida
1	Mitchella repens
1	Morella cerifera
1	Nyssa sylvatica
1	Osmunda regalis
1	Panicum sp.
1	Persea borbonia
1	Pinus taeda
1	Prunus serotina var. serotina
1	Quercus falcata
1	Quercus laurifolia
1	Quercus nigra
1	Quercus stellata
1	Sassafras albidum
1	Smilax sp.
1	Symplocos tinctoria
1	Toxicodendron radicans
1	Vaccinium arboreum
1	Vaccinium corymbosum
1	Vitis rotundifolia
1	Wisteria sinensis
2	Acer rubrum
2	Aralia spinosa
2	Arundinaria gigantea
2	Campsis radicans
2	Chasmanthium laxum

Table B-2. Continued.

Sampling Location	Species
2	*Cirsium sp.*
2	*Diospyros virginiana*
2	*Eremochloa ophiuroides*
2	*Gaylussacia dumosa*
2	*Gelsemium sempervirens*
2	*Hypericum hypericoides*
2	*Ilex glabra*
2	*Ilex opaca*
2	*Ilex sp.*
2	*Ilex vomitoria*
2	*Liquidambar styraciflua*
2	*Magnolia grandiflora*
2	*Magnolia virginiana*
2	*Mitchella repens*
2	*Morella cerifera*
2	*Nyssa sylvatica*
2	*Parthenocissus quinquefolia*
2	*Paspalum notatum*
2	*Persea borbonia*
2	*Photinia arbutifolia*
2	*Photinia pyrifolia*
2	*Pinus taeda*
2	*Polypremum procumbens*
2	*Prunus serotina var. serotina*
2	*Quercus laurifolia*
2	*Quercus nigra*
2	*Rhus copallina*
2	*Rubus sp.*
2	*Sassafras albidum*
2	*Smilax rotundifolia*
2	*Symplocos tinctoria*
2	*Toxicodendron radicans*
2	*Unknown Cyperaceae*
2	*Unknown Lamiaceae*
2	*Unknown Poaceae*
2	*Vaccinium arboreum*
2	*Vaccinium corymbosum*
2	*Vaccinium elliottii*
2	*Vitis rotundifolia*
2	*Woodwardia areolata*
3	*Acer rubrum*
3	*Boehmeria cylindrica*
3	*Carex sp.*
3	*Carpinus caroliniana*
3	*Cyrilla racemiflora*
3	*Dulichium sp.*
3	*Fraxinus caroliniana*
3	*Hydrocotyle umbellata*
3	*Hymenocallis sp.*
3	*Hypoxis hirsuta var. leptocarpa*
3	*Ilex opaca*

Table B-2. Continued.

Sampling Location	Species
3	Liquidambar styraciflua
3	Mikania scandens
3	Nyssa biflora
3	Osmunda regalis
3	Pinus taeda
3	Quercus laurifolia
3	Smilax sp.
3	Sphagnum sp.
3	Taxodium distichum
3	Toxicodendron radicans
3	Vaccinium elliottii
3	Viburnum dentatum
3	Woodwardia areolata
4	Acalypha sp.
4	Acer rubrum
4	Ambrosia artemisiifolia
4	Aralia spinosa
4	Axonopus sp.
4	Bignonia capreolata
4	Campsis radicans
4	Chamaesyce sp.
4	Conyza canadensis
4	Cornus florida
4	Cyperus sp.
4	Desmodium sp.
4	Dichanthelium sp.
4	Diodia teres
4	Eremochloa ophiuroides
4	Erigeron vernus
4	Eupatorium capillifolium
4	Galium aparine
4	Gelsemium sempervirens
4	Gnaphthalium sp.
4	Hypericum sp.
4	Ilex opaca
4	Liquidambar styraciflua
4	Medicago sp.
4	Mitchella repens
4	Morella cerifera
4	Nyssa sylvatica
4	Opuntia sp.
4	Osmunda regalis
4	Oxalis corniculata
4	Parthenocissus quinquefolia
4	Paspalum notatum
4	Paspalum sp.
4	Persea borbonia
4	Pinus palustris
4	Pinus taeda
4	Polypremum procumbens
4	Potentilla canadensis

Table B-2. Continued.

Sampling Location	Species
4	*Quercus laurifolia*
4	*Quercus nigra*
4	*Quercus sp.*
4	*Rhus copallina*
4	*Rubus argutus*
4	*Solidago sp.*
4	*Stylisma sp.*
4	*Toxicodendron radicans*
4	*Unknown Lamiaceae*
4	*Unknown Poaceae*
4	*Vitis rotundifolia*
4	*Woodwardia areolata*
4	*Yucca sp.*
5	*Acer rubrum*
5	*Arundinaria gigantea*
5	*Betula nigra*
5	*Boehmeria cylindrica*
5	*Campsis radicans*
5	*Carex sp.*
5	*Chasmanthium laxum*
5	*Cyperus sp.*
5	*Cyrilla racemiflora*
5	*Fraxinus caroliniana*
5	*Fraxinus pennsylvanica*
5	*Gelsemium sempervirens*
5	*Hymenocallis floridana*
5	*Hypericum hypericoides*
5	*Hypoxis hirsuta var. leptocarpa*
5	*Ilex opaca*
5	*Ilex sp.*
5	*Itea virginica*
5	*Liquidambar styraciflua*
5	*Mikania scandens*
5	*Mitchella repens*
5	*Nyssa biflora*
5	*Onoclea sensibilis*
5	*Osmunda regalis*
5	*Panicum sp.*
5	*Persea palustris*
5	*Pinus taeda*
5	*Quercus laurifolia*
5	*Quercus lyrata*
5	*Sabatia sp.*
5	*Saururus cernuus*
5	*Scleria triglomerata*
5	*Smilax sp.*
5	*Sphagnum sp.*
5	*Taxodium distichum*
5	*Toxicodendron radicans*
5	*Triadenum walteri*
5	*Unknown Asteraceae*

Table B-2. Continued.

Sampling Location	Species
5	*Vaccinium corymbosum*
5	*Vaccinium elliottii*
5	*Vaccinium sp.*
5	*Woodwardia areolata*
5	*Woodwardia virginica*
Alt 1	*Acer rubrum*
Alt 1	*Aristida stricta*
Alt 1	*Arundinaria gigantea*
Alt 1	*Chasmanthium laxum*
Alt 1	*Clethra alnifolia*
Alt 1	*Cyrilla racemiflora*
Alt 1	*Gaylussacia frondosa*
Alt 1	*Gelsemium sempervirens*
Alt 1	*Hypericum sp.*
Alt 1	*Ilex coriacea*
Alt 1	*Ilex glabra*
Alt 1	*Liquidambar styraciflua*
Alt 1	*Lyonia lucida*
Alt 1	*Magnolia grandiflora*
Alt 1	*Magnolia virginiana*
Alt 1	*Morella cerifera*
Alt 1	*Nyssa sylvatica*
Alt 1	*Panicum sp.*
Alt 1	*Persea borbonia*
Alt 1	*Photinia arbutifolia*
Alt 1	*Pinus palustris*
Alt 1	*Pinus taeda*
Alt 1	*Pteridium aquilinum*
Alt 1	*Quercus nigra*
Alt 1	*Sassafras albidum*
Alt 1	*Smilax sp.*
Alt 1	*Symplocos tinctoria*
Alt 1	*Unknown Fabaceae*
Alt 1	*Vaccinium corymbosum*
Alt 1	*Vaccinium crassifolium*
Alt 2	*Acer rubrum*
Alt 2	*Arundinaria gigantea*
Alt 2	*Asplenium platyneuron*
Alt 2	*Callicarpa americana*
Alt 2	*Campsis radicans*
Alt 2	*Catalpa speciosa*
Alt 2	*Chamaecrista sp.*
Alt 2	*Cornus florida*
Alt 2	*Eupatorium capillifolium*
Alt 2	*Fraxinus pennsylvanica*
Alt 2	*Gelsemium sempervirens*
Alt 2	*Ilex glabra*
Alt 2	*Ilex opaca*
Alt 2	*Juncus sp.*
Alt 2	*Lespedeza sp.*
Alt 2	*Ligustrum sinense*

Table B-2. Continued.

Sampling Location	Species
Alt 2	*Liquidambar styraciflua*
Alt 2	*Magnolia grandiflora*
Alt 2	*Magnolia virginiana*
Alt 2	*Mitchella repens*
Alt 2	*Morella cerifera*
Alt 2	*Nyssa sylvatica*
Alt 2	*Osmunda cinnamomea*
Alt 2	*Parthenocissus quinquefolia*
Alt 2	*Paspalum notatum*
Alt 2	*Persea borbonia*
Alt 2	*Pinus taeda*
Alt 2	*Populus heterophylla*
Alt 2	*Prunus serotina var. serotina*
Alt 2	*Pteridium aquilinum*
Alt 2	*Quercus laurifolia*
Alt 2	*Quercus nigra*
Alt 2	*Rhexia virginica*
Alt 2	*Rubus sp.*
Alt 2	*Salix caroliniana*
Alt 2	*Sassafras albidum*
Alt 2	*Smilax sp.*
Alt 2	*Symplocos tinctoria*
Alt 2	*Toxicodendron radicans*
Alt 2	*Unknown Fabaceae*
Alt 2	*Vaccinium corymbosum*
Alt 2	*Vaccinium elliottii*
Alt 2	*Vitis rotundifolia*
Alt 2	*Woodwardia areolata*